This Book Graciously Donated By
The Women's Cancer Coalition

Give to Your Heart's Content
. . . Without Giving Yourself Away

Give To Your Heart's Content
. . . Without Giving Yourself Away

by Linda R. Harper, Ph.D.

Take Care!
Linda R Harper

Innisfree Press, Inc.
Philadelphia, Pennsylvania

Published by Innisfree Press, Inc.
136 Roumfort Road
Philadelphia, PA 19119
800-367-5872
www.InnisfreePress.com

This book is dedicated to my father,
James H. Harper,
whose giving heart continues to live on through the
many lives he touched.
Always there for me,
I know my Dad's spirit will continue
to accompany me on this book's journey
and throughout my life.

Acknowledgments

I am grateful to my great-grandmother, Harrie Vernette Rhodes, Thomas Moore, and Father Paul Keenan for their writings that inspired me while working on this book. A special thank you to Father Paul for his interest, encouragement, and especially his foreword.

An ongoing thank you to my mother, Mary Harper, who has always given so freely and joyfully. Thanks to my husband, Mario, for his support and ideas. Thank you to Steve, Sue, and Mike, and to every member of my family who gave their love and support through yet another book! A special thanks to my mother-in-law and father-in-law, Tina and Mike, for all they give so easily that allows me the time to write. A heartfelt thanks to my best friend, Sally, for her continual encouragement. A warm thank you to Michele for her enthusiasm, and to

Doris and Laura, who encouraged me to develop this book sooner rather than later.

Thanks to all of my clients, workshop participants, and readers of *The Tao of Eating* who contributed to this book's development. I am also grateful for my animal companions, who give from their hearts so naturally. Many thanks to Dr. Sheila, Betty, Sheila, and everyone at the Cat Vet and Sanctuary for giving me the opportunity to give to *my* heart's content. And thank you to my father's doctors, nurses, and hospice workers—true role models for soulful giving.

A special thank you to my nephew, Ben Harper, for his on-call technical support, ideas, and help in editing my writing. Thanks also to Helane Hulburt for her editorial assistance. My deepest gratitude once again to my editor and publisher, Marcia Broucek, for being so easy to work with, for her wonderful understanding of soul, and for nurturing the seeds of this book. Thanks to the entire hard-working staff at Innisfree Press and to Sheila Orbach for her many creative ideas and efforts. Once again, my gratitude to Sara Steele for another beautiful cover.

Contents

Foreword

I n all the world there is nothing so bewildering and mysterious as the soul. Its ways are inscrutable, though its presence can be deeply known. When we think we have it figured out, it surprises us with a new turn of events that leaves us shaking our heads. Just when we're feeling so confused that we're sure we'll never know anything for certain again, someone—a stranger, a neighbor, an enemy—will come along with the help or the suggestion that sets us free.

The lenses through which the soul views life often enable us to see by first dismantling our ordinary vision. At the bidding of the soul, those who were strangers amazingly know precisely where we live and claim a place in our hearts. People whom we regarded as helpers and intimates suddenly take a separate path. An old temptation suddenly blazes into full-blown allurement, while a long-standing passion somehow fails to excite us any longer.

Myriad are the ways of the soul and labyrinthine its paths. If we try to ignore it, it is liable to seek us out; and if we try to force it to do our bidding or to stay within the limits that we set for it, it will elude us as deftly as the criminal dodges the detective.

We observe the soul in much the same way a scientist observes waves and particles: by glimpsing its effects and its path. We do not see it directly, but sense where it has been and what it has done there. Thus we see intimations of qualities such as character, intelligence, discernment, purpose, faith, hope, and love. Humor and sadness, too—and the greatest teacher of all: soul-inspired confusion. It is by indirection and suggestion that we know the soul; yet by another of its ironies, the more we come to know it, the more we long to. Its elusiveness creates an allure, and—so long as we do not make overmuch of this—a kind of talent for perceiving it.

To the soul, there is no distinction to be made between giving and receiving. We think of them as opposites, but the soul is totally at home with reconciling things we believe to be opposites. We normally conceive of giving and receiving in terms of material things and attributes; and even when we try to apply the concepts to intangible things, we still manage to treat them like matter.

As we normally think of giving, it involves our letting go of something and presenting it to someone else. If I give you a book or a sum of money, I no longer have it and now you do. In that sense, I have less and you have more. Most of us, even very wealthy people, are careful about naming the beneficiaries of our financial largesse. Beyond a certain point, we know, we could end up with no money at all. Giving has its limits. If I give you a job, I can't give it to someone else, at least until another position opens up. There are limits when it comes to the giving of material things. At least, we normally think so.

Because we tend to think in terms of matter, we tend to think of less tangible things as quasi-material, and therefore limited in supply as well. If I give you an hour of my time, I can't give it to someone else. Eventually, we can become frustrated by our perception that we have precious little time in which to get all of our tasks accomplished. Love can become a limited commodity: we eventually learn to apportion our love to those who give to us in return. We invest our love, as we invest our money, where we think we will receive the most for our investment. We often speak of "using up" our energy. We run and run, until, like the gas gauge in our car, we find ourselves "on empty." We lament that we have given all of our energy away to others, and now, we cry, there is nothing left. We are exhausted.

Because the soul does not deal primarily in material things and attributes, it has a very different way of viewing giving and receiving. The soul believes that what is most real is not in limited supply, cannot be exhausted, and cannot be lost, missing or depleted. The realities of the soul—life, energy, beauty, truth, goodness, love, and so forth—are essentially eternal. You don't lose or deplete your supply of them when you give them away. While our ordinary minds balk when someone tells us to love our enemies or to do good to those who hate us, the soul knows that it does not lose love when it gives it away. It is natural for the soul to give love and natural for the soul always to have love. It is the same with our experience of time and eternity. Thinking in our usual concepts, we can readily lament "wasted years," "missed opportunities," and "stupid decisions." Without comment, the soul instead takes our past moments for what they are, draws wisdom from them as the bee draws pollen and eventually honey from the flower, and, thus enriching us, leaves all else behind and draws us forward. Indeed, the soul invites us to rest when we feel tired, but with a view to drawing upon its infinite resources rather than just taking a break from exhaustion.

There are many of us for whom the lessons of soulful giving are uncharted territory. Because of habit or real or imagined necessity, we have driven ourselves to the point of physical and/or emotional depletion. Linda Harper's *Give to Your Heart's Content* shows us practical ways in which we can transition from the usual ways of looking at giving, to the broader and wiser ways of the soul. In a straightforward but gentle manner, she guides us to an understanding of the unique styles of giving we have personally adopted, and shows us options that will help us bring the soul to bear upon the choices we make as to how, when, and what to give. From her vast background as a practicing psychotherapist and from the deep resources of her heart, she guides us toward setting limits that will enhance the soulfulness of our giving, while gently expanding our capacity for generous giving, both to others and to ourselves.

If you feel trapped in your patterns of giving, Linda Harper will introduce you to a new level of freedom. You will be surprised that giving to yourself and caring for others go hand in hand, and even more surprised to learn how much more soulful and enriched your own life can be.

You have a treat in store. Be ready for some happy surprises.

—Father Paul Keenan,
Author of *Good News for Bad Days,*
Stages of the Soul, and *Heartstorming*

Introduction

$\mathcal{M}$ost of us aspire to become more giving people. We want to be good and caring. We teach our children not to be selfish, to share and give freely to others. But too often we find ourselves saying "yes" to requests when we really want to say "no," and our giving becomes a forced act. We want to "do the right thing" but end up feeling exhausted as we try to squeeze one more act of giving into our busy days. Our ambitions become a set-up for feeling inadequate. Our strained efforts block the natural flow of giving from the soul.

When we give, we often evaluate the experience—consciously or unconsciously—with one of these questions:

- Was my gift recognized and appreciated?
- What did I get for my efforts?
- What did I accomplish?

What we do not realize is that these questions contain a fundamental flaw: They focus on *outcome*, on the results of our actions.

Outcome-oriented giving produces three kinds of unnatural givers: the TRADER, the MARTYR, and the CONTROLLER.

- The TRADER gives expecting something back and feels resentful when the exchange does not seem fair.

- The MARTYR ignores personal needs in order to please others and is disappointed when the sacrifice goes unnoticed.

- The CONTROLLER gives expecting to see particular results and is frustrated when things do not turn out as planned.

By focusing on outcome, all three of these givers deprive themselves of the full meaning and joy of giving. Outcome-oriented acts of giving lack soul because the giver's fulfillment depends upon external events. Most of us have experienced this loss of soul that comes from outcome-focused giving.

Ancient scriptures remind us that the core of giving lies deep within the heart. Or, as Paul simply states in his letter to the church at Corinth, "God loves a cheerful giver" (2 Corinthians 9:7).

When the soul, our innermost essence, is allowed to be present, joyful giving can be a natural part of our everyday life. The soul wants no external rewards; its pleasure lies within the process itself. It experiences all aspects of life wholeheartedly from a deep place within, completely engaged in the experience at hand. From this perspective, giving is not a skill to master or a rare talent, but a way of the soul that each of us can discover and allow to unfold.

A return to soulful giving begins with an understanding of the soul's needs and desires, and a willingness to consider them in the daily choices we make. I call these challenges of the soulful life the "Three A's": Authenticity, Acceptance, and Appreciation.

> *Authenticity.* The first challenge is to live, and give, in ways that are consistent with who we really are, in sync with our true nature. Soulful giving occurs when our innermost essence, our unique and deepest self, is an integral part of the act.

> *Acceptance.* The second challenge is to accept both the good and the bad things that comprise our lives, and embrace what is presently here. Soulful giving celebrates the meaning of the ordinary events of life.

> *Appreciation.* The third challenge is to appreciate the complexities of the human experience and allow life to unfold. Soulful giving uncovers the intrinsic joy and pleasant surprises within the experience.

Give to Your Heart's Content . . . Without Giving Yourself Away is not about giving more or giving less. It is about giving authentically, from your deepest self, from your soul. Giving wholeheartedly with no strings attached, no expectations. Giving that nurtures rather than depletes. Giving that flows freely and fully because the giving process itself is energizing, pleasing, and replenishing.

Give to Your Heart's Content offers a five-lesson guide that will put soul back into your experiences of everyday giving. Each letter of G.U.I.D.E. stands for a key lesson to understanding the heart of soulful giving:

Give wholly to yourself.

Unconditionally choose to give.

Integrate your unique gifts.

Delight in the act of giving.

Experience the expanding capacity to give.

Each of the five chapters offers contemplative exercises to help you personalize your everyday giving. As you become the giver you were meant to be, you will deepen the meaning of your life through soulful, ordinary acts of giving—to yourself and others. There is no greater joy than giving from the heart!

LESSON I
Give Wholly to Yourself

Compassionate toward yourself
you reconcile all beings in the world.

*T*he first step on the path to becoming a soulful giver is to nurture yourself.

Taking care of yourself may seem like a basic and natural act, but it is surprisingly difficult for many of us to do—especially on a daily basis. Self-giving is one of the first things we stop doing when the demands of life overwhelm us. We feel pressured in our society to achieve. We feel the need to use our time efficiently to "get things done"—usually by completing a task, creating something, or solving a problem. And since self-nurturing does not often result in a product, we let it fall to the bottom of our list of priorities.

Cultural Factors in Not Giving to Yourself

In our culture both women and men have been discouraged from self-giving. Christiane Northrup, M.D., an expert on women's health and author of *Women's Bodies, Women's Wisdom,* describes our culture as one that teaches women that they must "sacrifice themselves and their needs for the good of others."[1] She believes that our society encourages women *not* to give themselves what they need.

Stephanie Golden, Ph.D., author of *Slaying the Mermaid: Women and the Culture of Sacrifice,* finds that

> in our culture, suffering is a crucial component of the sacrifice expected of women[2] . . . There can hardly be a single woman in our culture who hasn't struggled with the conditioning that tells her she's no good unless she consistently disregards herself to put other people first.[3]

In his book *Knights Without Armor,* Aaron R. Kipnis, Ph.D., a specialist in depth psychology and gender issues, looks at similar challenges for men. He explains that a man's underlying belief that he is loved only for what he can provide keeps men habitually taking care of others' needs at the expense of their own. He describes the tendency of men to extend themselves beyond the natural limits of their "bodies, hearts, and minds in an attempt to achieve some ideal of manhood and productivity."[4]

Not only are men discouraged to nurture themselves, Dr. Kipnis explains that

> if a man is sensitive to the needs of his body and emotions, he will not be acknowledged by his culture as manly.[5]

Another influence that interferes with self-giving is the parental voice in our heads that says, "Don't be selfish." I cannot tell you how many times in my clinical practice I have heard my clients express this fear of being selfish! While Webster's definition of selfish is to be concerned exclusively or excessively with one's own needs while disregarding others, many people feel that they are being selfish if they do not always put another person first or if they take anything "extra" for themselves.

One of my clients, Ruth, related an incident in her life that exemplifies this fear of selfishness. One day Ruth canceled an appointment for her massage when, at the last minute, her daughter called and asked her to babysit her grandchildren because her daughter wanted to run some errands. My client felt she would have been a "selfish mother" if she turned down her daughter's request.

I also felt this pressure of not being a "giving enough" person when I declined to give a monetary pledge to a cause that was not particularly dear to my heart. The phone solicitor accused me of not "caring about people." Had I given a donation in attempts to convince the caller I was not a selfish person, it would have been a self-depleting and inauthentic act of giving for me.

Not giving according to someone else's wishes does not make a person selfish or self-centered.

Many people think that "self-nurturing" means being "self-centered." In truth, self-centered actions are usually not self-nurturing because they fail to consider the desires of the whole person, especially the desires of the soul. In his book *Care of the Soul,* Thomas Moore describes narcissistic or self-seeking behavior as a signal that the soul is not being loved.[6] It can be a selfish act not to replenish ourselves with what we need because we can then never be the givers we were meant to be!

The Natural Way

"We are part of a vast web of relationships and inter-relationships which sing themselves in the ancient harmonies."[7] As Madeleine L'Engle has observed so often, physicists who study the microcosm are discovering that nothing happens, nothing exists, in isolation. Every being and every action are interconnected and part of the greater whole. Throughout her writings, Madeleine L'Engle celebrates this "butterfly effect":

> In a recent article on astrophysics I came across the beautiful and imaginative concept known as "the butterfly effect." If a butterfly winging over the fields around Crosswicks should be hurt, the effect would be felt in galaxies thousands of light years away. The interrelationship of all of Creation is sensitive in a way we are just beginning to understand. If a butterfly is hurt, we are hurt.[8]

From this perspective, giving to ourselves is a part of nurturing others. As Pema Chödrön, an American Buddhist nun, describes it:

> What you do for yourself—any gesture of kindness, any gesture of honesty and clear seeing toward yourself—will affect how you experience your world . . . What you do for yourself, you're doing for others, and what you do for others, you are doing for yourself.[9]

It is the natural way of soulful giving to nurture ourselves. As the soul is replenished, its capacity to give will expand. We see the connection between self-giving and nurturing others in animal behavior. Animals in the wild listen to their instincts to find food for themselves, leaving their crying offspring behind.

Their natural act of self-nurturing is necessary so they can feed and nurture their young.

Pet owners often experience this reciprocal relationship between self-giving and nurturing with their animal companions. My dog, Blackie, listens to his innate need for affection and plops himself on my lap. Quite often, he appears at a time when I really need some love and affection but think that I am too busy to stop and pet him. His ability to respond to *his* needs fulfills both of us.

The hummingbird is also a wonderful example of the natural relationship between self-nurturing and giving. Listening to its instincts, a hummingbird consumes sweet nectar from flowers four to eight times an hour. While nourishing itself, pollen falls on the hummingbird's body. This unconsumed pollen pollinates the next flower the bird visits, causing new flowers to grow. In nurturing itself, the hummingbird gives back to the world.

The natural interconnectedness of giving is also revealed in the hummingbird's relationship to flower mites. These tiny insects live only in flowers from which the hummingbird feeds. When flowering ceases, the mites need to find new homes but are unable to proceed on their own to other flowering plants. They ride inside the nostril of the hummingbird who is pursuing its own nourishment while traveling from flower to flower. What an amazing example of nature's proof that listening to one's innate needs provides for others!

So is the natural flow of giving revealed in the way of flowers. The process of producing seeds that, in turn, give life to more blooms is a stunningly simple example of self-nurturing that keeps on giving. Each flower has its unique needs that allow it to thrive and give life to other blossoms. The daffodil, for example, will turn itself toward the sun to receive the rays of nourishment it needs to thrive. But it must also give of itself in order to rejuvenate. A gardener knows that when a daffodil's blooms have faded, and its leaves have yellowed and dried, the bulb is ready to be divided in order to create new flowering plants. The gardener also knows to separate only the bulbs that come apart easily: The natural way of the flower is to give of itself when ready, not when it will cause depletion. In giving of themselves, the flowers flourish year after year, creating new blooms to continue the process.

The Necessity of Self-Giving

"Life is difficult" is the first line of the first chapter in Scott Peck's well-known book *The Road Less Traveled*[10]—and a good reason to take care of ourselves. We need every possible resource to deal with many of the challenges and unexpected hardships that life often brings. Many times clients have told me that they felt at the "end of their rope" . . . and then one more troublesome life event happened. When we let ourselves run so close to empty, we have no fuel left for those unexpected situations that seem to arise. I am reminded of the airline attendant's safety instructions: In case of an emergency, put on your own oxygen mask first so you can help those who may need your assistance.

Although we may believe our neglect of self-care is a gift for others, our sacrifice often results in depriving those very persons we are trying to nurture. One of my clients who lost her husband described him as a "self-sacrificer, overdoer, and someone who always put his family first." His doctor believed that his death from a heart attack may have been avoided had he listened to his body's symptoms and taken some preventive self-care measures. My client's husband gave to others, but by not taking care of himself, he is no longer around to give at all.

I have also heard stories of individuals who became sick or even died while caregiving for a relative with a serious illness because they did not adequately take care of themselves. When a loved one becomes sick, caregivers too often ignore their own needs to take care of what seems to be the more important needs of others. But in reality, this is a time when self-care is crucial to caring effectively and empathically for someone else. Since we need an energized body to care for others, we must be aware of and attend to our unique physical needs, which include nourishment and rest. It is just as important to pay attention to our emotional needs so we have the inner resources to creatively problem-solve the everyday situations that arise.

 Taking Responsibility for Self-Giving

Have you noticed how often we look for encouragement from others before allowing a gift to ourselves? We take along a shopping buddy who will give us permission to buy something we like. It is easier to stay in bed an extra few minutes in the morning if our spouse is also not rushing out of bed to begin the day's projects. We will consider having dessert if our dinner partner tells us, "Go ahead . . . live it up!" We consult with others about taking days off, going on vacation, hiring help . . . the list is endless. Somehow it feels less self-indulgent if somebody else condones or approves of our actions.

Soul-centered giving asks that we courageously take charge of our own self-care by trusting our ability to consider what is necessary. Taking care of ourselves is a gift of freedom we give to those who care about us. When we are in touch with what we need, others are freed of that burden. In her discussion of "heartfullness" in her book *The New American Spirituality*, Elizabeth Lesser describes the gift that self-giving is to others:

> Your self-knowledge and self-love are the most unselfish gifts you can give to another. Self-knowledge makes you clear, strong and trustworthy and allows others to know where you stand. Self-love makes love of others more genuine.[11]

An example of this gift to others is illustrated by my client Pat in her relationships with two friends. She described her friend Jill as easy to be with because Jill was not afraid to express what she wanted to do. Pat described her other friend Sara as someone who was very giving in their relationship, but quite private about what she needed. While Pat enjoyed Sara's company, she often wondered if her friend was enjoying herself or just going along with what Pat wanted to do. Pat found herself looking for some signs from Sara and trying to second-guess her needs during their time together.

When we meet our own needs, we also give others permission to give to themselves. We demonstrate that self-givers are not selfish, but are able to give more in their interactions with others. We give children an opportunity to see that it is a good idea to listen to their inner needs. An example of the importance of modeling self-giving is illustrated by Carol's story. Carol was a client of mine who did not sit down at the dinner table. She cooked meals for the family and then ate standing by the counter overlooking the table, so she was readily available to get anything else a family member might need; more water, an extra napkin, a second helping, etc. As she and I explored the option of sitting with her family, I discovered that she had grown up with a mother who was also "on-call" during dinner and did not nurture herself with the full experience of a sit-down family dinner. When she realized that she was following her mother's example, Carol made a decision to model a different way for her children.

Giving to the Whole Person

Who knows your particular needs better than you do? As Henri Nouwen discusses in his book *Reaching Out: The Three Movements of the Spiritual Life,* it is our responsibility to listen to the wisdom within:

> The development of this inner sensitivity is the beginning of a spiritual life. It seems that the emphasis on interpersonal sensitivity has at times made us forget to develop the sensitivity that helps us listen to our own inner voices . . . discover the voice telling us about our inner necessity . . . [12] No friend or lover, no husband or wife, no community or commune, will be able to put to rest our deepest craving for unity and wholeness.[13]

When we integrate the needs and desires of the whole person—the body, mind, and soul—we unlock the natural flow of giving and receiving. Meaning and pleasure flow throughout each act. For example, a fully nourishing gift to myself is a walk in the forest preserve. It satisfies my physical desires for movement and fresh air, my mind's wishes for a healthy form of stress-relief, and my soul's longing for a simple pleasure that connects me to the world of nature.

When our choice to give to ourselves does not nurture the whole person, we limit our capacity to be more giving to others. Working out on a treadmill at a health club, for example, may satisfy our physical desires for exercise but ignore the soul's desire for beauty. Eating a nutrition bar "on the run" may satisfy the need for physical nourishment but leave the soul's desire for pleasure and celebration unfulfilled.

In a society that has not encouraged us to hear our soul's wishes, we may find that many of the gifts to ourselves only respond to our physical needs, making soulful giving to others much less accessible. Imagine preparing a meal for someone else while you are starving! Likewise, the soul must be fed to energize its natural desire to give.

Integration of the desires of our whole person needs to be a daily occurrence. Allowing yourself one week of vacation to recuperate after a year of overwork and self-neglect does not replace wholly giving to yourself daily.

My client Georgia believed in the value of self-nurturing, but would wait until she "got everything else done first" before giving to herself. She had to find a way to give to herself more freely and regularly. Her solution was to write down simple pleasures and small comforts on thirty-five slips of paper. Some of these included taking a bubble bath, eating a rich piece of chocolate, buying flowers, taking a walk. She placed these slips of paper in a beautiful antique bowl—a present from a favorite aunt. Every Friday night, she would take a slip from the bowl and then engage in that activity—without guilt. Making self-giving a ritual has helped Georgia follow through with replenishment for herself. The bowl's prominent place on her dresser is also a daily reminder of her commitment to taking care of herself. Georgia has found that she has much more energy and enthusiasm for her classroom on Monday morning when she enjoys one of her "small comforts" on the weekend.

Since giving to ourselves is a necessary part of life, there are consequences to ignoring this natural way of things. Our society has lost the art of natural self-giving, so many of us are unaware of the parts of ourselves that lack nourishment. We attribute the signs to other causes. If we pay attention to reoccurring symptoms, we may find that they are expressions of a neglected inner self. As Thomas Moore, in his book *Care of the Soul*, states, "When soul is neglected it doesn't just go away, it appears symptomatically in obsessions, addictions, violence and loss of meaning."[14] He suggests that we "look to our physical problems for guidance in aligning our lives with our nature."[15]

Do You Need Gifts from Yourself?

Take a look at the following self-inventory. These are common symptoms that are signals that you are in need of self-giving.

Rate yourself from 0-3 on the degree to which you experience these symptoms that may be expressions of the unmet needs of your body, mind and soul. Use the following rating system:

0 = rarely or never

1 = once in a while

2 = often

3 = almost always/constant

BODY SIGNS

_____ Tension

_____ Excessive fatigue/exhaustion

_____ Body aches such as headaches and tired muscles

_____ Rashes and hives

_____ Trouble sleeping

_____ Lack of energy and enthusiasm for starting your day

_____ Fast heart beat and feeling "hyper"

_____ Upset stomach

_____ Trouble getting up in the morning

_____ General physical discomforts

_____ BODY SUBSCALE SCORE

MIND SIGNS

_____ Crabbiness

_____ Hostile feelings toward loved ones

_____ Feelings of resentment

_____ An overfocus on past hurts

_____ Anger outbursts

_____ Absentmindedness, inability to focus or concentrate

_____ Making more careless mistakes/more accident prone

_____ Forgetfulness

_____ Lack of clarity about personal goals

_____ Uninterested in events in your present life

_____ MIND SUBSCALE SCORE

SOUL SIGNS

_____ Vague feelings of emptiness

_____ Reoccurring disturbing dreams

_____ Fantasies about escaping your present life situation

_____ Fantasies of a new love relationship that will ignite a
current life that feels dull

_____ Excessive overeating

_____ Compulsive behavior such as drinking, gambling,
or sexual behavior

_____ Living in and glorifying the past

_____ Not feeling like yourself

_____ Feeling alienated from others

_____ Lack of everyday enjoyment

_____ SOUL SUBSCALE SCORE

_____**TOTAL SIGNS SCORE**

Each BODY, MIND, and SOUL SCORE will range from 0 to 30. The higher the score, the greater your tendency to express your unmet needs through that domain—body, mind and/or soul.

Interpreting your TOTAL SIGNS SCORE

There are many reasons that your body, mind, and soul may be displaying symptoms of discomfort, and the necessary medical and professional consultation, evaluation, and intervention should always be obtained. This self-inventory is not a substitute for medical diagnosis. It is simply a way for you to begin to pay attention to what your inner wisdom may be telling you.

Your TOTAL SIGNS SCORE will range from 0 to 90 and indicates the degree to which your body, mind, and soul are presenting you with signs to pay attention to their needs and desires. The higher your score, the more likely you are in need of self-nurturance in your everyday life.

0 to 10 points: None or few
You pay good attention to your need for self-nurturance.

11 to 30 points: Mild
You are displaying some signs that you need to give more to yourself every day.

31 to 60 points: Moderate
There are many indicators suggesting that your lack of attention to your own needs is contributing to an overall lack of well-being.

61 to 90 points: Strong
You have lost touch with your own inner wisdom telling you what your basic needs are. You are in strong need of self-nurturance to replenish your presently depleted self.

Contemplations for Rediscovering Self-Giving

- ✦ Look over the symptoms that received your highest scores. Can you remember what kinds of changes in your life occurred at the same time these symptoms began?

- ✦ Trust your intuition. What do you think each symptom may be telling you about what you need? What is stopping you from fulfilling that need?

- ✦ It is not always a simple matter to discover a need and meet it. Can you explore a gradual change that you can make to help yourself get what you need? Try it, and note what happens to your symptoms.

- ✦ Think of a common way that you give to yourself. Describe the gift and your reaction to it. Does it fulfill your body, mind, *and* soul? If not, what can you do to make it more of a "whole person" gift to yourself?

Ten Simple Ways to Practice Giving to Yourself

In the following chapters, we will explore ways to allow your unique style of giving to unfold naturally. The following ideas, however, are gifts of self-nurturing that replenish everyone. Feel free to alter them or expand on the ideas to fit your unique needs. Get yourself into the habit of incorporating self-giving into your everyday life . . . beginning today!

1.   Give yourself the gift of doing one thing at a time.
Next time you are thinking about trying to do two or more things
at the same time, stop and choose to fully immerse yourself in
one activity at a time. If one task has to wait until a little
later—let it wait. Enjoy a more relaxed, focused experience.

2.   Give yourself the gift of a few minutes alone just to SIT.
Decide to take time out of your schedule and do nothing for at
least ten minutes. Just sit. Let your mind become empty. You
might be surprised to find what "nothing" has to offer!

3.   Give yourself the gift of stretching a self-imposed deadline.
Find one of the "shoulds" you have placed upon yourself that has
a time constraint. Consider stretching your time limit a few more
hours or another day. Do you *really* have to have it done in such
a hurry, or can you complete the task at a slower and more enjoyable pace?

4.   Give yourself the gift of being human.
So you made a mistake. Apologize or make amends if necessary,
and then let go of it. Allow yourself to be human without self-
degrading yourself for the error.

5.   Give yourself the gift of saying "no."
Many of us have days fully packed to the brim, yet we add one
more thing when asked. That "one more thing" can be the difference between an enjoyable busy day and a busy day filled with
pressure. Stop and allow yourself the option to politely say, "No,
not today."

6.   *Give yourself the gift of slowing down.*
Many of us are in the habit of going through our days at an accelerated speed. Make the effort to reduce your rate of movement. Slow down when you get dressed, eat, drive, or walk from place to place.

7.   *Give yourself the gift of NOT doing something.*
Whether your list of things to do is on paper or in your head, choose something from it and decide you are not going to do it today. In reality, we rarely get everything done from our lists, anyway. Decide to skip mowing the lawn, or making the phone call, or filing the papers, or vacuuming the house today. Make this decision early in your day so you can enjoy the sense of freedom in having one less thing to do.

8.   *Give yourself the gift of going out of your way for a special nurturing eating experience.*
Rather than grabbing fast-food or putting that pre-made meal in the microwave, stop and ask yourself, "What would I really like to have that would fulfill my whole person: body, mind, and soul?" Take time out to nurture yourself with a delicious and nutritious meal in a soul-nourishing atmosphere.

9.   *Give yourself the gift of simple comforts.*
There are many basic pleasures in life that nurture our bodies while feeding our souls. Consider the "little things" that can make your day more comfortable. Most of us already know what they are, but we do not stop and take the time to add them to our day. These personal comforts might include slippers, flannel sheets, pajamas heated up in the dryer just before bed on a cold night, an extra pillow, a long bath, hot apple cider, a glass of ice

water with a slice of lemon, a favorite snack, or a scented candle. Of course, the list is endless. If you are not sure where to begin, start by looking at one of the many books describing the simple joys of life and try a few that appeal to you.[16] The idea is to create your own unique and ever-changing list and to keep these gifts to yourself readily available.

You also may want to make your own Small Comforts Kit, like my client Georgia did. Write down on small slips of paper some simple pleasures and small comforts that you enjoy. Put them in a container that you create or that holds special meaning to you. Keep your Small Comforts Kit in a prominent place to remind you to take care of yourself. Create your own ritual for drawing the slips of paper and giving yourself a gift on a regular basis—without guilt.

10. *Give yourself the gift of not asking someone for permission to nurture yourself—just decide to do it.*

The next time you feel indecisive about giving yourself a gift, decide that you do not need to have somebody else tell you it is okay to have it. Give yourself the chance to make this decision on your own. You are reaffirming your faith in your natural ability to provide self-nurturing.

LESSON II
Unconditionally Choose to Give

She has but doesn't possess, acts but doesn't expect.
When her work is done, she forgets it.
That's why it lasts forever.

*T*he second lesson of soulful giving is to give unconditionally, with no strings attached.

The soulful giver has no prerequisites or expectations of getting something back in return. However, we live in a society of deal-making where rewards and benefits are continually used to motivate people. This conditions us to expect equality and fairness in our giving. When we give a gift, we may consciously or unconsciously be thinking about "keeping things even." This is a set-up for disappointment. When we give a gift expecting something of equal value in return, we are left guiltily waiting for repayment. When we don't get what we think we deserve, we have robbed ourselves of the true joy of giving.

When we are focused on getting a fair deal or a fair exchange, the "Trader" in us is trying to avoid being slighted, taken advantage of, or forced to carry an unfair burden. Most of us have experienced this Trader within. Take the following Quick Quiz to discover how much the Trader may be affecting your views about giving.

How Does the Trader Affect You?

PART I

YES   NO

_____ _____ 1. Do you prefer giving to yourself after you have earned it?

_____ _____ 2. When you give yourself something "extra," do you typically try to make up for it later?

_____ _____ 3. Before buying yourself a gift, do you often ask, "Do I *really* need this?"

_____ _____ 4. Do you get impatient with yourself if you are feeling down for no apparent reason?

_____ _____ 5. Is it hard for you to ask a favor that you may not be able to return?

PART II

YES   NO

_____ _____ 6. When given a gift, do you try to give one back of equal value?

____ ____   7. Is it difficult for you to accept a gift that is of greater value than the one you gave?

____ ____   8. Do you often experience disappointment when you do not get an expected present?

____ ____   9. Do you sometimes experience resentment in having to give because somebody gave to you?

____ ____ 10. Do you feel guilty if you do not give a gift to someone who gave one to you?

PART III

YES   NO

____ ____ 11. Do you worry about being taken advantage of?

____ ____ 12. In a personal relationship, are you uncomfortable giving out more love than you are getting?

____ ____ 13. Do you guard against becoming vulnerable in your intimate relationships?

____ ____ 14. Do you often weigh out the costs and benefits before making a decision to give?

____ ____ 15. Do you often wait until others express love first before you show your love for them?

____ ____   **TOTAL TRADER (T) SCORE**

Score one point for every question you answered "yes." Add all of your points together to obtain your Trader (T) score. Your total score will range from 0 to 15. Your T score shows you to what degree you may knowingly or unknowingly be influenced by the mind set of a Trader in your everyday giving experiences to yourself and others.

Analyzing your Trader Score

0 - 2 points = Unconditional Giver
The Trader is seldom present in your giving experience. You are able to give without focusing on the external rewards. You enjoy the pleasures and depth of meaning that comes with giving freely and unequally.

3 - 6 points = Mild Influence
You have experienced the joy of giving with "no strings attached." Some of your choices to give, however, are influenced by a concern for what is fair and just when giving of and to yourself.

7 - 10 points = Under the Influence
Although you are aware that focusing on the rewards of giving leads to disappointment and resentment, it is difficult for you to give to yourself and others unless it makes logical sense. You are missing out on some of the simple joys of random, unrewarded, and unequal giving and receiving.

11 - 15 points = Trader
Your present satisfaction in giving to others strongly depends on what you receive back. You seldom freely give to yourself, and your gifts to others may often feel forced. You probably experience resentment, disappointment, and a feeling that you are often carrying the greater load.

Interpreting your Trader Score
Your T score reflects the degree to which the beliefs of a Trader influence your giving style. A high score does not mean you are a person who lacks generosity. Rather, a high score reflects the problems inherent in giving with rewards and payback in mind.

Analyzing Your Subscale Scores

To understand more fully how the Trader in you is affecting your giving, take a few more minutes to look at three areas that may be blocking you from unconditional giving.

Give yourself one point for every "yes" in Part I.
This is your <u>Undeserving Self</u> score.

Give yourself one point for every "yes" in Part II.
This is your <u>Just Rewards</u> score.

Give yourself one point for every "yes" in Part III.
This is your <u>Holding Back</u> score.

For each subscale, your score will range from 0 - 5. Take special note of the subscales where you have the highest score. These represent the greatest obstacles between you and unconditional giving.

0 points = No interference.
This obstacle is not interfering with soulful giving.

1 to 2 points = Some interference.
You may have some behavior and thoughts of this obstacle that keep you from unconditional giving.

3 to 5 points = Interference.
You are aware of the effects of this obstacle when giving to others and when neglecting your self. Consider questioning the beliefs that go along with this obstacle so that you can rediscover unconditional giving.

Three Obstacles
to Unconditional Giving

Let's look at each of the obstacles that maintain the Trader in your giving experiences.

1. The "Undeserving Self" Obstacle

The Undeserving Self subscore looks at the conditions we often require before we are willing to nurture ourselves. Traders feel that they must earn their gifts, atone for them later, or resist them—unless they determine that these acts of self-giving are a necessity. Guilt and rationalization often accompany the Trader's self-gifts.

For example, John is in the process of refinishing his family room and has trouble freely giving himself a break. He only allows himself a Saturday afternoon nap if he agrees to work late into the evening or already has accomplished "extra" tasks the night before. He also feels that he must justify the afternoon rest, so he compares the amount of sleep he gets to others, and he feels guilty if he hears about people who put in longer work hours.

Traders often struggle with freely giving themselves a gift they want. Do you often consider questions like these when deciding to nurture yourself?

- Do I really need this now?
- Can I live without it?
- Do I deserve to take that right now?
- Have I earned this?
- If I give this to myself now, how can I make up for it later?

These questions illustrate attempts to justify acts of self-nurturing, which diminish the pleasure from these gifts.

Sometimes we ask others to support our reasons before we will give ourselves what we want. Rather than taking responsibility for decisions about self-giving, Traders often put their friends in the difficult position of justifying their actions for them. Many of my married clients struggle with this. They want approval for the things they desire, and they attempt to get it by giving their spouses lists of reasons to prove that they deserve or have earned a particular gift. Why do we need somebody else to tell us that our giving equation makes sense? Must gifts to ourselves be based on logic?

Listening to society's values on "fair deals" is one of the reasons that many of us fall into the trap of Trader when trying to decide what we will give ourselves. For example, one of my clients chose to take two weeks of her vacation after the loss of her sister. She needed to give herself more time than the policy of her workplace allotted, but was concerned that she might be seen as a weak person for "taking more time off than most people." Another client works for a company that gives their employees five days of leave time for bereavement. Rose preferred to go back to work immediately after her mother's funeral, but she was concerned that others would think she was "hard-hearted" because she did not take her expected five days. For Rose, returning to work was the true gift to herself.

When we self-give, it is important to allow ourselves what we truly need, based on who we are, rather than comparing ourselves to the needs of others or accepting a standard established by someone else.

2. The "Just Rewards" Obstacle

Another hindrance to unconditional giving is the underlying false belief that we should "keep things even" when giving. In other words, we believe that when we give to others, we should receive a gift of equal value in return. Or, if others give to us, we should give equally in return. But people, life, and the world do not follow this order.

"Getting our fair share" detracts from our ability to immerse ourselves in replenishing experiences. When I was in college, it was common for a few of us who were studying late to share the cost of having a pizza delivered. It seemed like some of the pizza eaters were so concerned about getting their money's worth that they gobbled the pieces so fast they couldn't possibly have enjoyed the texture and taste of the pizza, or the sociability of the late evening get-together. Their attitude detracted from the nurturing experience for everybody.

We can see this overfocus on what is fair by watching children take turns with popular video games. There is often a child so consumed with making sure he or she is getting a turn equal to the previous child that they miss out on the pleasure of actually playing, as well as the fun of watching others play.

Expecting "just rewards" leads to three kinds of ungratifying giving experiences: disappointment, waiting for what we think we deserve, or feeling guilty for not giving our fair share.

Disappointment: Expecting a gift or a reward of equal value frequently results in disappointment. My client Martha agreed to help out on some projects at work because putting in extra time in the past had resulted in a large bonus. After six months of overtime, her boss presented her with a $500 gift certificate and two airline tickets. Unfortunately, Martha felt that her work was worth much more than that, a feeling exacerbated by the fact that she had no interest in traveling and was afraid to fly. She was not only disappointed but felt undervalued as an employee and began to question the value of her work. As Martha did, Traders often degrade their own self-worth. When they do not receive what they had anticipated, they decide that their act of giving must not have been "good enough."

Sometimes disappointment occurs when we expect a similar gift in return but receive something quite different. This kind of unsatisfying exchange occurred with Nancy when she bought her boyfriend, Tom, an engraved gold bracelet. Nancy hoped he would follow her example and present her with a personalized piece of jewelry. Tom, however, had his own ideas for a gift and gave her a year's membership at the health club she frequented. Nancy was disappointed because she wanted something "more intimate" from him. Since she rarely spent money on jewelry, but considered her club membership a necessary expense, her boyfriend's gift did not feel special to her.

Waiting: If we anticipate "just rewards" for our act of giving, we often fritter away time and energy waiting for the reward to arrive. When my client Jane, for example, works into the evening, she expects her boss to reward her with a day off. She spends an extra few minutes every night at the office, dropping hints that she deserves an extra vacation day. Her boss, however, sees after-hours as part of the job and chooses to reward Jane with praise and positive evaluations. Another client, Harriet, complains that her neighbor never returns the numerous favors she has done for her. On every holiday and special occasion she waits to see if her neighbor will pay her back with a gift of gratitude. She is disappointed and then begins waiting again for the next possible day her neighbor might reciprocate with a gift.

The dissatisfaction that occurs when we give because we are counting on future rewards is illustrated by the turn of events in my client Marilyn's life. When her spouse became disabled at an early age, she not only experienced significant distress from his injury, but resentment and disappointment. Marilyn felt that she had been giving more than her fair share for the past ten years. She had continued her uneven giving because she expected her husband to reciprocate "in a few years" after he got his business going. Then he would have more time and money for her. When Marilyn realized that the future she had expected to "even things out" was not going to happen, she felt angry about "the ten years she wasted."

Feeling Guilty: Another common problem with "just rewards" giving is the pressure it can place on others and ourselves to participate in unwanted gift giving. Many people complain about the length of their list of holiday gifts to buy. Attempting to give a gift of equal value to the one received can be a hardship for persons with limited budgets. Some of my clients report anxiety over trying to keep track of who gives them what, such as the value of birthday presents their children receive, so that they can give the "proper amount in return." Others describe feeling overwhelmed by the task of keeping up with expected reciprocal gift-giving, and then feeling bad about themselves for finding the giving process such a burden.

The idea of having to keep gifts "even" also results in guilty feelings for those who receive a present that costs much more than the one they gave. It works the other way, too. There have been times when I have found the "perfect gift" but was afraid to give it to my friend because I knew she would feel that she must reciprocate with a gift of equal value. The joy of giving from the heart gets lost in calculations and equations.

3. The "Holding Back" Obstacle

A common way we deprive ourselves of the full pleasure of unconditional giving is to hold back our gifts of love. We conserve our expressions of affection to avoid getting hurt or to keep from becoming too vulnerable. When we try to give only under "safe" conditions, however, we deprive ourselves of the intrinsic joy that the giving of unconditional love offers.

Society's promotion of the "rules of romance" hinders unconditional love. Love is often discussed as a game to be played strategically for a winning outcome. The "love experts" suggest that individuals seeking a long-term relationship should ration out their calls, compliments, and gifts so as not to appear "too interested." Many of my clients struggle with how much to give in their interpersonal relationships. They often ask themselves (and me) the following questions:

- Am I giving too much?
- Am I being taken advantage of?
- Will my mate lose interest if I give too easily?
- Are my gifts being taken for granted?
- Am I being a sucker?
- Am I getting enough in return?

A young woman I saw named Betsy spent many therapy sessions discussing her concern that she might be scaring men away because of her tendency to give too much. She thought that she should "play hard to get," but when she tried to hold herself back, she felt like a "phony." When she accepted that she was comfortable being an outgoing and warm person, she decided to continue to be herself and enjoy her ability to give, regardless of how it might be misperceived. Although this decision appeared to make Betsy more vulnerable to rejection, she no longer judged herself or regretted her behavior. Her confidence in her authentic self was strengthened, regardless of the outcome. She eventually became involved in a fulfilling relationship with a man who appreciated her open and natural manner.

Since it is energy-consuming to restrain our natural inclinations to express love, holding back can result in an inhibited style of living where many loving opportunities pass us by. For example, my client Julie decided not to call Michael, the man she had been dating for a couple of months, even though she wanted to continue seeing him. She felt that he had not displayed an equal amount of interest in her, since she did most of the calling. After not dating for about a month, they happened to run into each other in a store. Michael seemed happy to see her and had apparently misinterpreted her lack of calling as a loss of interest. Protecting himself from rejection, he had decided not to call her. Attempting to follow the love game's rule of "playing it cool," both had held back their natural inclinations and were missing out on time together that they both desired.

When we hold back our love to avoid being hurt, we end up depriving ourselves of the pleasure of giving. I think of my client Susan who enjoys giving little gifts to others, such as a note in a lunch box, a card, loose change in someone's pocket, etc. She became involved with a man who not only did not share this interest but also neglected to remember the "big things," such as anniversaries, birthdays, and romantic holidays. Susan feared that her excessive giving would scare him away. She decided, however, not to hold back her authentic way of relating and loving—while at the same time accepting his way—and to live with what happened.

 ## Four Secrets of Unconditional Giving

The key to unconditional giving is acceptance. Accepting who we are. Accepting who others are. Accepting what *is* without trying to change it. Accepting the irregularities of all aspects of life—including our acts of giving. Once we embrace acceptance, we are released from restrictions on our giving. Gifts offered in the spirit of acceptance deepen the meaning and enhance the pleasure experienced in that moment of giving.

1. Accept yourself unconditionally.

The first secret of unconditional giving starts with an unconditional acceptance of our innermost essence. This free acceptance
of our unique nature fuels our ability to truly give to others.
When we allow our own idiosyncratic feelings, we can more easily accept the uniqueness of others.

Jean is an elementary school teacher whose story illustrates
the connection between acceptance and unconditional giving.
Jean recognizes that meeting new people is stressful for her.
Rather than denying this discomfort or degrading herself, she
accepts this attribute and nurtures herself by limiting the
amount of time she spends in these situations. She gently challenges herself at a manageable pace. This self-understanding enhances her ability to meet new parents and to help students with
similar shynesses. Acceptance of the way she is expands Jean's
capacity to unconditionally give to others.

Unconditionally accepting ourselves means being willing
to work with all the different parts of us that we might find. For
example, there may be times when we are bubbling over with
excitement at the chance to give, and other times when we follow through with a commitment to give, but a heavy heart detracts from the pleasure. Accepting the wide range of emotions
and reactions that we experience as we give to ourselves and others helps to prevent criticism and fault-finding from robbing us
of the joy and meaning these acts of giving offer.

I think of my client Carol who had trouble accepting the
lack of joy she felt caring for her cats after one of them passed
away. She was self-critical and felt guilty because she did not enjoy the time she spent with the other cats. As she began to accept
that the grief over her feline companion who passed away was
presently shutting down her affection for her other pets, she was
able to lift her own harsh self-judgment and feel better about
herself.

Accepting ourselves also includes accepting the person we were in the past. This is a difficult gift for so many of us to freely give, especially when it includes forgiveness for prior actions we may regret. We need to realize our humanness, accept that we make mistakes, and let go. Punishing and judging ourselves for our past only consumes our energy, makes us feel bad, and feeds our beliefs that we are inadequate givers. When we embrace who we have been, we are free to fully explore our experiences, learn from our mistakes, and open our hearts to possible ways we may now want to change present behavior. Accepting all of who we are and have been will expand not only our ability to give to ourselves, but our capacity to give forgiveness and acceptance to others.

2. *Accept the natural inequalities of life.*

The second secret of unconditional giving lies in acknowledging the unevenness of life's situations. The challenge of acceptance is recognizing that the natural flow of life is not necessarily logical and fair, and finding pleasure in gifts even when they have not been "earned" or might not be reciprocated.

One of my clients was contemplating how much time to spend with her in-laws, considering that her husband did not attend *her* family's gatherings. She realized she still wanted to enjoy his family's get-togethers, even though it felt "unfair" that her husband was not spending the same amount of time with her family. If she had focused only on keeping things equal, she would have missed these soul-nourishing occasions and the deep friendship she unexpectedly formed with her husband's sister.

Another of my clients demonstrated unconditional giving by continuing to create holiday greeting cards for all of her family even though her brother never reciprocated the gesture or even acknowledged her efforts. She keeps on expressing her creativity and maintaining this family tradition. If she decided to stop because of her brother's lack of response, she would be blocking an avenue for her soul's expression. Instead, she chooses to accept her brother's nature while continuing to deepen her own authenticity.

When we fail to let go of the resentment caused by a focus on "fair" and "even," we short-change ourselves. I think of my experience of walking my dog. During one period in my life, I was begrudgingly taking her for a walk every night, feeling that I was doing an unequally large share of the care of our family pets. When I chose to let go of my resentment and concentrate on the experience, however, I discovered that this evening walk that I had been deploring was a calming, peaceful time with my dog and a chance for me to enjoy the outdoors. With a new perspective, I realized that these walks were replenishing. My previous focus on equality was stripping me of the natural joy I could receive by fully absorbing the present experience.

Acceptance sometimes means dealing with events that unexpectedly interfere with our giving intentions. For example, if you are planning on participating in a charitable walkathon and it is pouring rain, you can accept the weather, your disappointment, and then look at the options of unconditional giving that are open to you: You can accept your reluctance to be wet for the next three hours and give yourself the gift of staying home, or you can recognize that the rain may add an unpleasant dimension to the event but decide to keep your commitment. The key is to attempt to struggle honestly with all of your feelings as you make the decision that is right for you.

This challenge of acceptance also includes the understanding that our ability to give varies and can change with circumstances and events. We might give to someone who never gives back to us, or who repays us twenty years later. Or perhaps, receivers of our gifts never have the chance to give to us, but are able to give to another because of our gifts to them.

Acceptance asks us to realize that the irregularities of life can be a burden, especially when we choose to make a sacrifice. Individuals who find themselves in the role of caregiver for a seriously ill or disabled loved one are often called to let go of their expectations of fairness in life and sense of equality between effort and reward. My client Maria faced this struggle when her mother became sick. Maria had put off starting a family to pursue higher education. When her mother's illness required intervention, Maria suggested that her two siblings share with her the responsibility of their mother's care. But her brother and sister each had a new baby at home and felt they did not have the time, space, or money to care for their mother as well. Maria felt she was being asked to make unfair sacrifices. But in accepting the nature of the situation, she saw that she had two choices: postpone her educational goals and care for her mother, or place her mother in a nursing home. Although she had hoped the responsibility would be divided equally, Maria realized that no fair deals were going to be worked out. She decided to accept the situation, take on the greater share of her mother's care, and delay her schooling.

Sometimes giving unconditionally means acknowledging that we are in a situation with no good options; we must accept the circumstances that have arisen as we make our decision about giving. The challenge of acceptance means accepting our true feelings—our hesitancies and resentment—yet still embracing our decision to give.

When we are challenged to give unconditionally, sometimes the only reward we experience comes from the strength we find within, choosing to be true to ourselves and to make sacrifices for a greater good.

3. Give love freely.

The third secret of unconditional giving is unconditional love. Rabbi Harold Kushner describes this power in *Handbook for the Heart*, when he says,

> None of us has the power to make someone else love us. But we all have the power to give away love, to love other people. And if we do so, we change the kind of person we are and we change the world we live in forever.[17]

In other words, we need to stop worrying about equality in love and open ourselves to the unique ways each person gives. Love cannot be objectively measured. Many variables influence each person's capacity to give. What might be a difficult and strong act of love from one person may be a common everyday occurrence for another.

For example, for some individuals, saying " I love you" is an easy gift of love they offer daily, while others muster up all of their courage to get the words out every once in a while. Tongue-tied lovers may freely show their feelings by giving in other ways that come more naturally to them, but these gifts may be overlooked if our heart is set on receiving love our way. An overfocus on the need for equality in giving can blind us to the unique ways love may be given. Ancient philosopher Lao Tzu asks us:

> Can you love people and lead them without imposing your will? Can you deal with the most vital matters by letting events take their course?[18]

When we let go of expectation, we open to whatever gifts may come. Although many of us feel it as a vulnerability, giving love freely strengthens, not weakens, our capacity to love. My client Angie struggled with this when her natural desire to give conflicted with her fear of being hurt. While touring England,

Angie took photographs of places special to her. Among them was Stonehenge, and she wanted to share her Stonehenge pictures with someone who would appreciate the structure's beauty and mystery. The one person she knew who had expressed a similar wonder in Stonehenge was her co-worker, Connie. Angie was reluctant because Connie has slighted her in the past, but she decided to share her pictures anyway. It ended up being the beginning of an unexpected close friendship.

Unconditional gifts of love come in all shapes, sizes, and packages. Give a compliment to a friend just because you thought of it. Tell her that you enjoy her sense of humor, his ability to problem-solve, or her laid-back attitude that relaxes you. Let the clerk know that you appreciated his persistence or pleasant nature. Give somebody a hug, a kiss, or a pat on the back "just because." Give words of encouragement. Perhaps you could allow a friend under stress to be out of sorts, a little crabby or unthoughtful. A listening ear is a valuable present that everyone of us has to offer. Give somebody the chance to vent even when you see things differently. Once in a while try letting your mate have the last word or even do most of the talking.

Try giving the gift of letting something go, rather than scolding or even mentioning the other person's oversight or error. This idea of "keeping things even" often keeps futile arguments going on and on as each person continues to support his or her side of the story. Hurtful words are reciprocated with more hurtful words. Why do we think one offensive remark deserves another? Stop and think about what you might be willing to give to yourself or the other person instead of continuing fruitless exchanges.

Some simple and free gifts include:

- allowing mistakes
- letting somebody be human
- accepting the eccentricities of others
- giving others space

- giving somebody a little time to be late, too slow, or too fast
- ignoring an annoying habit
- accepting other people's inability to give to us according to our wants.

When we find courage to give love our own way and not let the limitations or giving styles of others inhibit what we authentically want to give, our capacity to love grows with each unconditional gift we give, regardless of outcome.

4. Give "recklessly."

The fourth secret of unconditional giving is to give with total abandon. Don't hold back waiting for the "right" conditions. In other words, perhaps this is not the best time and was not in your original plan to give, but go ahead and do it anyway. Let reckless giving interfere with your scheduled day, and enjoy the spontaneity of your choice.

Since both my husband and I are pet lovers, I'll tell you two of our "hero" stories. My husband once stopped his car on the way to work in a driving rainstorm to rescue a turtle that had been hit by a car on a busy highway. He could have easily justified looking the other way for a number of logical reasons: he would be late for work, the turtle might already be dead, he might not be able to get it before it got hit again, and he would be putting himself in a somewhat risky situation. He chose, however, to follow his impulse and, with the help of a vet who performed emergency shell repair, the turtle still thrives today.

Sometimes, the opportunity for spontaneous giving appears just when you would rather it didn't, but this may be just the right time to go for it! I recently saw a lost dog walking the streets as I was driving into work for a fully scheduled evening of appointments. While the part of me that felt already "too busy with important commitments" wanted to look the other way, I gave in to the urge to complicate my evening, and I picked up the dog. I called the phone number on his tag, but the place of business was closed. He hopped in my car and stayed at the office and then spent the night at my house. The next morning I was able to contact his owner, and after feeding the dog a big breakfast, and buying him a stronger collar and an ID tag with his place of residence, I made a two-hour round trip and delivered my animal friend to his home. I don't believe the dog ever realized he was even lost or endangered, and so he showed me no particular signs of appreciation. The owner, who was rather gruff and a little suspicious of me, never even uttered a word of thanks. Nevertheless, as I drove away, I felt a deep sense of fulfillment and joy. I remembered that I had been worrying about something before I noticed the dog, but that anxiety was now replaced with a sense of well-being and inner peace.

We are often inspired by stories of reckless giving by heroes who choose to abandon logic and endanger their own lives to give a stranger a remote chance to live, even when conditions look hopeless. Whether your spontaneous decision to give puts your life at risk—or only delays your day's plans—the principle is the same: Give of your full self without calculation of your investment or your compensation, without measuring the risk or return.

 ## Ten Ways to Practice Giving Unconditionally

1.   Give yourself some unearned gifts.
Consider starting out your morning with compliments to yourself or affirmations of self-acceptance. What are some positive

statements you could make about yourself before you have done anything yet to "deserve" your praise?

2. *Give a random act of kindness.*

Arrange an act of giving where you cannot possibly expect anything in return. The pure joy in a random act of kindness comes from the unlikelihood that you could get anything back from the recipient of your gift. While I was on tour at a bookstore in Ohio, I had a pleasant conversation with a woman whose book I had signed at my table. A few minutes later while I was talking with someone else, she put an inspirational card and a twenty-five-dollar gift certificate for the bookstore on my table. She left quickly and only signed the card, "Sue," so I was unable to even send her a note of appreciation.

There are endless random acts of kindness; you can find examples and ideas throughout the *Random Acts of Kindness* series by Conari Press. For example, tell someone in line to go ahead of you for no reason or let the other person take the last free sample available even though you were there first. One anonymous act of giving I enjoy is putting quarters in expired meters—it is especially rewarding when the person with the ticket book in hand is readily in sight.

3. *Accept a gift you will not reciprocate evenly.*

You just received an extravagant gift from someone to whom you have never given such a present. Accept it graciously, say thanks, and then fully enjoy it without guilt or thought of equalizing the gift.

4. *Ask for a favor with no thought of returning it.*

Many of us are often reluctant to ask a favor if we do not feel we have one coming or we are not sure that we can reciprocate in a timely manner. Go ahead and ask anyway. Let someone else have the pleasure of giving unevenly to you with no expectation of a reward.

5.   *Give forgiveness to a loved one.*

Decide to give forgiveness to someone who has hurt you. Don't deny the pain you experienced, but give unearned forgiveness. Waiting for someone to atone for their actions often results in feelings of impatience, wondering, measuring, and never feeling like "enough" has been done to make up for what you have been through. Freely offering your forgiveness releases you from the hold the hurtful act may have had on you and allows you to feel the strength in your ability to give from within.

6.   *Purposely give unevenly.*

I enjoy giving food servers large tips, especially when they have been exceptionally attentive or friendly. Sometimes, however, it can be fun to give a generous tip to a waiter or waitress who seems preoccupied or crabby. I prefer to leave before it is seen so as not to elicit an apology or excuse for their unfriendly service. You might also try giving a service person a tip who is not expecting one. Sometimes I tip the person who packaged my carry-out food. My mother enjoys talking to children with lemonade stands about the plans they have for their afternoon's earnings and then handing them a ten-dollar bill for a quarter's worth of lemonade. Whether they take the money calmly or jump for joy, my mother finds giving to the children pleasurable and fulfilling.

Another example of giving unevenly is purposefully not getting the lowest price for a negotiable purchase. When you buy a painting at an artists' market, consider paying the price that the buyer is asking. You don't have to try to get it cheaper just because that is the way it is usually done. It also doesn't have to mean "you got taken"; perhaps you simply chose to give the artist the price he or she felt the painting was worth.

7.   *Give and receive from a new perspective of inequality.*

Don't think of yourself as a sucker for giving too much, but appreciate your ability to give unevenly or unrewarded. Consider more creative uneven ways to share gifts. Have you spent a lot of time and energy making and revising plans to "fairly divide household chores" and still felt the division of labor was uneven? Try looking at these duties as gifts that can be given to yourself and to each other. Consider the talents and preferences of each family member and match the gift of housework with each person's natural inclinations. Consider giving your children a "free day" each week in which they can choose to skip their assigned daily chores for no reason at all.

8.   *Give differently than usual.*

Go ahead and decide to give in an atypical way. I remember one Christmas having so much work to do that I did not send cards to my friends—an activity that I usually enjoy doing. With my workload more manageable by February, I had the time to really enjoy creating gifts, so I decided to send handmade Valentine's Day cards.

9.   *Give yourself the full pleasure of the unexpected gifts that life sometimes presents.*

Give yourself the pleasure of indulging in some of the natural ways of the world that appeal to you. As you accept the nature of things, enjoy the rare warm day with an extra walk or a longer stay in the park. Embrace the unexpected snowstorm that strands you in your home and snuggle by the fire with a good book. Don't fight the traffic jam and the fact that you are going to be late; relax and enjoy the time alone to unwind, reflect, or listen to music.

10. *Stop giving in some manner that you presently do to keep things even.*

Is there some giving routine that you feel you must do that you find unfulfilling or irritating? Question whether you really need to keep putting the time and energy into keeping things even in a giving situation that has become draining for you. Decide to give yourself the gift of letting it go. I know that parents often fall for their teenagers' arguments that they are not being treated fairly. While it is important to acknowledge children's feelings, gifts do not have to meet others' expectations of what is fair, or any expectations at all!

Rewards of Unconditional Giving

✧ Unconditional giving is unlimited. You freely give what you want and are not dependent on a person or event to allow it.

✧ With less of your time and energy focused on the logistics of the gift-giving exchange, you have an opportunity to live life more fully.

✧ You experience the pure pleasure that giving offers.

✧ With no expectations, you are often pleasantly surprised as gifts come back to you.

✧ You promote self-acceptance and acceptance of others in an often critical world.

⊹ As you accept the unevenness of life, you have a more honest appreciation of all the things that make up life and increase your ability to cope with the unexpected.

⊹ You experience new pleasures when the focus on external rewards is removed.

⊹ You feel the strength in giving your way, regardless of the outcome.

⊹ You feel the power of love when it is given freely, even if it is not appreciated, and your capacity to love continues to grow.

⊹ You enjoy the unique pleasures that only uneven giving can offer.

⊹ You enjoy the replenishment you experience by unconditionally giving to yourself.

⊹ The more you accept, the more you unconditionally give. As you increase acts of unconditional giving, you become more accepting.

⊹ You feel the strength that accompanies the ability to be vulnerable when freely giving your love.

⊹ Unconditional giving is everlasting. When there is no expectation of a payback or external reward, the pleasure in the act lives within and can never be taken away.

⊹ The depth and meaning that is added to your daily life when you offer an unconditional gift becomes part of who you are. It grows and becomes part of the whole workings of yourself, your relationships, and the world.

Contemplations
for Rediscovering Unconditional Giving

✦ What gifts are difficult for you to give to yourself freely?

✦ Under what circumstances are you most likely to look for others' approval before allowing yourself a gift?

✦ What feelings do you often have that are difficult for you to accept as part of yourself?

✦ How can you allow these feelings to be part of you?

✦ What social expectations affect your gift-giving? Do you want to continue to go along with them or make some changes?

✦ What current life situations ask you to give unevenly?

✦ Think of the natural ways that you give love. Do you hold back because of your fear of being too vulnerable or giving too much? How can you begin to reclaim your authentic giving style?

✦ Describe a random act of kindness you have given. How did it feel?

✦ Describe a random act of kindness you have received. How did it feel?

LESSON III
Integrate Your Unique Gifts

Knowing Yourself is true wisdom.

*T*he third lesson of soulful giving is to integrate your uniqueness into your giving.

To be soulful givers, we need to honor the soul's desire for authenticity. What I mean by that is including all of our individuality—our strengths, weaknesses, vulnerabilities, and eccentricities—in our gifts and our style of giving.

When we ignore our individual uniquenesses, we fall into the trap of giving what we think someone else wants of us, in order to get recognition or approval. We give because we think we "should," or we give out of guilt. We may think we are doing something good by putting the other person "first," but when we ignore our own needs to make others happy, disappointment and exhaustion are sure to follow. Not only do we end up depleted, but the recipient feels the underlying pressure that comes with our gift: that we have made a sacrifice for them for which payment will be extracted at a later date.

When obligations rule our offerings, the "Martyr" in us feels drained by the perceived demands of others. The Martyr feels unappreciated as silent sacrifices go unnoticed. Most of us have experienced this interference from the Martyr within. Take the following Quick Quiz to discover how much the Martyr may be present in your views about giving.

How Does the Martyr Affect You?

PART I

YES   NO

_____ _____ 1. Do you often feel guilty when you nurture
                  yourself?

_____ _____ 2. Do you regularly feel depleted and exhausted
                  at the end of the day?

_____ _____ 3. Do you often ignore your physical needs (such
                  as drinking water, eating, using the bathroom,
                  or sleeping) when you are busy doing things for
                  others?

_____ _____ 4. Do you usually do what the "other person"
                  wants to do when planning an activity?

_____ _____ 5. Do you usually feel that doing something for
                  someone else should come before doing
                  something for yourself?

<u>PART II</u>

YES   NO

____   ____   6. Do you have giving habits that you keep because you have *always* done things that way?

____   ____   7. Are you disappointed in yourself when you feel anger or resentment when giving to a loved one?

____   ____   8. Do you generally feel like you should try to be a more giving person?

____   ____   9. Do you frequently give to others because you believe nobody else will?

____   ____   10. Do you commonly give to others because they expect you to?

<u>PART III</u>

YES   NO

____   ____   11. Do others repeatedly tell you that you do too much?

____   ____   12. Is it hard for you to ask for a favor?

____   ____   13. Have you been told by a doctor, therapist, co-worker, parent, friend, or significant other that you need to take better care of yourself?

____   ____   14. Do you wish others would notice or acknowledge your efforts a little more?

____   ____   15. Do you find yourself "dropping hints" in hopes that others would see that you need help?

____   ____   **TOTAL MARTYR (M) SCORE**

Score one point for every question you answered "yes." Add all of your points together to obtain your Martyr (M) score. Your total score will range from 0 to 15. Your M score shows you to what degree you may knowingly or unknowingly be influenced by the mind set of a Martyr in your everyday giving experiences to yourself and others.

Analyzing your Martyr Score

0 - 2 points = Authentic Giver
The Martyr is seldom present in your giving experiences. You are willing to listen to your inner voice and nurture yourself by integrating the needs of your body, mind, and soul. You enjoy giving to others in ways that express your unique traits. Your integrated gifts reaffirm your sense of self and enhance your natural ability to give.

3 - 6 points = Mild Influence
Your giving choices are influenced by a desire to please others. You may not realize that you are neglecting aspects of your true nature in your acts of giving to others, or in your lack of giving to yourself.

7 - 10 points = Under the Influence
Many of your acts of giving are tainted by the need to please others. You resist allowing yourself to fully and freely meet your own needs.

11 - 15 points = Martyr
Most of your giving experiences neglect your authentic nature. Your focus on pleasing others is usually at your expense and theirs. Your gifts to others often feel forced, depleted of energy, and unfulfilling. You need to look at your own nature and allow replenishment through self-nurturing.

Interpreting Your Martyr Score

Your M score reflects the degree to which the beliefs of a Martyr influence your giving style. A high score does *not* mean you are a person who is unable to give comfortably and happily to others. Rather, a high score reflects the problems inherent in giving that is focused on pleasing others.

Analyzing your Subscale Scores

To understand more fully how the Martyr in you is affecting your giving, take a few more minutes to look at three areas that may be blocking you from authentic giving.

Give yourself one point for every "yes" in PART I.
This is your <u>Self-neglec</u>t score.

Give yourself one point for every "yes" in PART II.
This is your <u>Shoulds</u> score.

Give yourself one point for every "yes" in PART III.
This is your <u>Mind Reading</u> score.

For each subscale, your score will range from 0 - 5. Take special note of the subscales where you have the highest score. These represent the greatest obstacles between you and authentic giving.

0 points = No interference
This obstacle is not interfering with soulful giving.

1 to 2 points = Some interference
You may have some behavior and thoughts of this obstacle that keep you from authentic giving.

3 to 5 points = Interference
You are aware of the effects of this obstacle when giving to others and when neglecting your self. It is important to pay extra attention to questioning the beliefs that go along with this obstacle so that you can regain integrated giving.

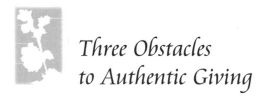

Three Obstacles to Authentic Giving

Let's look at each of the obstacles that maintain the Martyr in your giving experiences.

1. The "Self-Neglect" Obstacle

The first obstacle to authentic giving is the tendency to ignore our unique needs. Since the Martyr's focus is on pleasing others, self-nurturing is not a priority because it does not produce the immediate outcome of making others happy. Because Martyrs try not to spend time giving to themselves, they do not spend time looking within. Without this nourishment for their authenticity, Martyrs become depleted when they give to others, and also drain others around them.

Take a look at five conditions of giving to the self that is typical of the Martyr:

Self-giving "out of desperation": Martyrs will finally give to themselves when they are completely overwhelmed. The body runs out of energy from days or weeks of being overrun. Unable to get out of bed, the exhausted giver is forced to rest. As soon as physically possible, however, they often resume the same lifestyle that landed them in bed.

Many of my clients who are consumed with taking care of others report that they often go all day without eating because they cannot fit it in their day. Sometimes it takes the feeling of lightheadedness to convince them that they must find time for nourishment. Even then, rather than taking the time to nurture themselves with a nutritious meal, they fuel themselves with the closest, fastest food they can find—and usually eat it quickly while doing some other activity. Although a physical need is met, they get little, if any, enjoyment from the meal, and no replenishment for the soul. They also give themselves and others the message that they are less deserving of care than others.

The Martyr is not the only one who suffers from this form of self-neglect. When you give to yourself only "out of desperation," it places an uncomfortable burden on others. Friends and relatives feel bad, and oftentimes responsible, that the Martyr "overdid it." Sometimes they get put in the position of picking up the pieces when the exhausted giver falls apart.

June's story is an example of the way the self-neglecting giver burdens others. June was one of my clients who worked hard at her job, never took a lunch break, and rarely gave herself a bathroom break. She felt as if the entire survival of her department depended on her actions. The more she did, the more others expected her to do. To please others she continually added more responsibilities to her workload. When one of her co-workers needed to take a three-month leave of absence, June took over all of her duties. When the co-worker resigned rather than returning to work after the three months, June's boss decided it was not necessary to replace her since the work was getting done (by an overworked June). June was working beyond one person's capacity, but inadequately doing the work of at least two persons. June developed pneumonia with complications of a kidney infection and was unable to work for six weeks. Her doctor told her that not drinking enough water during the day and infrequent bathroom breaks contributed to her kidney condition. Meanwhile, on the job, other workers were stressed because the boss saw no need to replace June's position since the last time an employee took a leave, it appeared that no one new needed to be hired. Now, the office was in turmoil, morale was at an all-time low, and the work was not getting done. In spite of June's self-sacrificing efforts, the other employees were angry and blamed her for leaving them unprepared and overworked.

June's neglect of her own needs in order to please others back-fired.

Self-giving with an authority's permission: Martyrs will give to themselves when they feel they must because someone in authority, such as a doctor, therapist, or boss, has recommended it. When I was away at college, for example, I remember calling my parents many times and reporting that I was exhausted and stressed-out. They usually responded by suggesting that I take a night off from studying, which was just what I needed to do to take care of myself. Certainly I could have come up with that obvious solution, but I wanted their permission to give myself a break. Asking for authorization to self-give implies that we do not trust our own self-knowledge. We also place an unfair responsibility on others to interpret our signs of depletion and figure out what we need. When we do not take responsibility for our self-care, we set others up for misdiagnosing our needs and offering inadequate solutions.

Self-giving in secrecy with guilt: Martyrs restrain from self-nurturing because they want their energy to be devoted to pleasing others. When they do give themselves a break, a snack, or a pleasurable moment, they often try to keep it hidden, as if they were ashamed of their behavior. Two common examples of secret gifts to the self are nap-taking and eating snacks. I knew a person who put her special treats down the clothes chute and ate them privately while doing the laundry. A client of mine told me that she never eats chocolate in front of other people because she is afraid they will think she is being self-indulgent. Taking an afternoon nap also seems to be one of those pleasures readily admitted by few. It is usually justified with statements such as, "I wasn't feeling well so I laid down for a few minutes." My client Susan feels guilty watching certain daytime television soap operas. She recently married a man who told her that he thinks these programs "are a waste of time," so she tapes them and tries to watch them when her husband is not home. If he does walk in, she quickly changes the channel. She does not feel comfortable freely giving herself this pleasure.

Self-giving when you "happen to go along": Martyrs may try to nurture themselves by going along with somebody to whom they are giving. It may not be just what they need or at the best time, but it is a way of getting a little something for themselves while appearing to be concerned for others. For example, people have told me that they would "never cook just for myself," but they would prepare their favorite foods if there were others who would enjoy the meal.

An incident from my own life illustrates the way we may unknowingly try to get what we want by tagging along with a gift we are trying to give to others. On one of the first nice spring days of the year, my sister and I decided it would be fun to spend the day with her kids at a large amusement park. Looking back now, I can see that she and I were both desiring a relaxing day outdoors and some time to talk with each other. Deciding to "do something fun for her kids" was a way to give ourselves that gift incidentally. When two of the children said that they would rather go to a movie and stay inside, we were surprised, disappointed, and a little angry. "How could they *not* appreciate what we wanted to do for *them*!" Our hopes of doing something fun for ourselves by escorting the kids caused us to react strongly when the kids expressed a different preference. We could still have chosen to listen to our authentic desires, but we would then have had to admit it was to please us, not the kids.

I was counseling Maryann, a single mother, who explained that her feelings were hurt one evening because her teenage daughter did not want to go out to dinner. So Maryann stayed home, fixed both of them dinner, but then resented her daughter for spending the evening on the phone. "Why would she turn down a wonderful meal at her favorite restaurant just to talk on the phone?" she asked. "She doesn't appreciate anything I do." Maryann really needed a night out where someone else cooked and served the meal, but she could not freely take that for herself. She attempted to nurture herself by giving her daughter the gift of going out for dinner. She needed to recognize her own desire to eat out, and just go—with or without her daughter.

Self-giving only after others have come first: Martyrs often take care of everyone else first before allowing themselves a gift. For example, I have seen many mothers take dessert only after everyone else has had as much as they wanted. A common scene in restaurants is a mother who does not order what she wants to eat because she plans to make her meal from the food the kids do not finish. Usually this ends up being items such as a half-eaten sandwich, crusts, a vegetable that has now become cold, soggy French fries—probably not items she would have chosen for herself.

Martyrs will usually take a turn at something only if everyone else already had at least one turn. Adhering to an "others first" policy, they will cancel their own plans if it interferes with others' plans. For example, my client Julie had a ticket to go to a concert with some girlfriends. When her boyfriend asked if she could help at the concession stand for his baseball team that same night, Julie quietly gave away her concert ticket. Her boyfriend did not know of her plans at the time, but found out a few months later, when during an argument she blurted out that she had given up her prized concert ticket to help him out. He told her he could have easily found someone else to work the concession stand if she had only told him she had other plans. Julie had felt that pleasing him was more important than following through on her plans, but her harbored resentment came out angrily a few months later.

2. The "Shoulds" Obstacle

The second obstacle to authentic giving is a forced list of "shoulds" that inhibits giving with individuality. There are two kinds of "shoulds" that motivate Martyr-giving: shoulds based on what you think others expect, and shoulds created by your own self-expectations.

Does any of the following assumptions about others' expectations sound familiar?

What others expect . . .

- He'll be mad if I don't do it.
- They expect it of me.
- I have always done it for her.
- That is what wives or husbands are supposed to do.
- She'll think I don't love her if I don't do it.
- That's the way the family has always done it.
- I have never turned her down before.
- He said if I really loved him, I would do it.
- They'll think I'm selfish if I don't do it.
- If I don't do it, they won't think I am a nice person.

When we respond to "shoulds" for the purpose of pleasing others, our gifts are based on our perceptions of what others expect, without considering what is authentic to us. For example, a husband sends flowers to his wife because he thinks she is counting on them. His own way of expressing love, however, may be doing something different that she might also enjoy. Listening to this internal "should" limits the giving experience for both of them.

What about expectations you have of yourself?

What I expect of myself . . .

- The person who had the job before me did it, so I must do it, too.
- If I don't, no one else will.
- My mother always did it, and her mother always did it, so I will, too.
- Since I am able to do it, I should do it.
- Others have done it, so I can, too.
- I shouldn't make such a big deal about it— just do it.
- If I am really a caring person, I would do it happily.
- I should do this first; my needs can always wait.
- Others have had to do more than this, so I shouldn't complain.
- I should just be thankful for what I have and not need more.
- I wouldn't be a nice person if I didn't give this way.
- I don't really need that for myself, so I shouldn't want it.
- It would be materialistic to give that to myself.
- I can go without it.

When you give to try to meet a self-imposed standard, you ignore your true feelings and try to be who you think you *should* be. I have counseled clients who made sacrifices for loved ones but were self-degrading because they were unable to give "with a smile." Rather than giving themselves credit for engaging in a difficult act of giving, they were disappointed in themselves for not having the saintly attitude toward giving that they expected themselves to have. Not allowing your true feelings deprives you of an easy way of nurturing your self.

In my practice I see many mothers filled with guilt and depleted of energy, as they recite their lists of "shoulds"—activities they believe are essential to being a good mother. Their statements include: "I filled in every page of the Baby Book for my first child, but I haven't been able to keep it up for my other children. I feel terrible!" "I am so tired in the evening, but I know I should read to my kids every night." "Mornings at our house are pretty hectic, trying to get everybody up and out for the day, but I know mothers are supposed to fix a hot breakfast for their children."

How often do you turn down a much-needed walk—or nap or lunch break—because you felt you "had" to finish something, whether it was an office project, the laundry, or bill paying? When you regularly respond to self-imposed "shoulds," you are setting unrealistic standards that not only are a set-up to feel bad about yourself, but also a guarantee to deprive you of the pleasure and replenishment in the acts of giving you do choose.

3. The "Mind Reading" Obstacle

The third obstacle to authentic giving is expecting others to read your mind and know what you need. Martyrs are frequently disappointed when friends and family do not pick up on their subtle hints for help. Mind reading is an unrealistic expectation we place on others and only promotes unnatural acts of giving while straining authentic relationships.

Have you ever been around someone and had the feeling that they wanted you to do something or say something, but you just couldn't figure out what it was? Individuals in healthy relationships assume that each person is taking care of his or her own needs, so many of the sacrifices the Martyr makes go unnoticed and unappreciated. For example, when a person cooks a meal consisting of food she does not like as she tries to give the family what she thinks they would enjoy, her family members end up unaware of her food preferences and may not even realize she is disregarding her tastes.

Children being cared for by Martyr-mothers are often confused and full of guilt when their mothers become depleted from a lack of self-nurturing. I was counseling Janine, a sixteen-year-old teenager, while her mother was being hospitalized for exhaustion. She told me that she felt guilty for not realizing that her mother needed help, but was also angry that her mother had never asked her for any assistance. Expecting children to mind-read their parents' needs is an unrealistic expectation that puts pressure and stress on everyday family life.

Would you enjoy a gift from someone who obviously needs the item herself? Have you ever received a gift only to discover later that it was a major inconvenience and sacrifice for the giver? It is an uncomfortable feeling that takes away from the pleasure of receiving a gift and often causes us to be more hesitant in our interactions with that person.

My client Martha related a story that illustrates the uneasy feelings experienced by the Martyr's receiver. Martha and her friend Shirley had spent the day shopping for a dress that Shirley needed for a formal party. They found a dress that both of them liked, and Shirley bought it for the upcoming event. Knowing that Martha also wanted the dress (the store only had one), Shirley told her that she found the same dress at another store and gave the one she bought to Martha. Months later Martha discovered that Shirley had not really found the same dress and that she had not attended the party for which she had originally wanted the special outfit. Martha felt angry and "duped" by Shirley's manipulation. She also felt bad that Shirley had given up the dress and missed the party. Shirley's intentions were to please Martha, but it only left Martha feeling "fooled, a little guilty, and just plain bad about the whole thing."

Receivers of Martyrs' gifts often pay for it later. The resentment that Martyrs sometimes feel when a sacrifice goes unnoticed, or when others do not read their minds, usually festers inside and then makes a grand appearance. Martyrs may pout or withdraw as they wait for others to figure out what they need. Or, at a much later time after the giving act is over, they reveal that they had given up something important to try to meet the other person's needs. In the midst of a heated argument, the Martyr might exclaim, "I gave up the chance of a lifetime because I thought you needed me to stay home" or "I never wanted to move into this house, I hated it, but I knew you loved it, so I did." Often the receiver hears about the martyr's suffering long after the fact, and after the situation cannot easily be changed.

Four Secrets of Authentic Giving

The key to giving freely is authenticity. Recognizing our uniqueness. Uncovering our natural styles. Integrating them into our everyday lives. When we embrace authenticity, we are not held back by the expectations and demands placed on us by ourselves and others. Gifts offered in the spirit of authenticity flow freely and naturally, while affirming who we really are.

1. Recognize and respect your unique limits.

The first secret of authentic giving is to recognize when your giving is depleting you. If you are thinking or feeling any of the following, you have probably overextended your personal limits:

- I hate what I am doing.
- I am so sick of this person (who I usually enjoy spending time with).
- I feel trapped.
- I dread going there.

- I wish I could leave it all behind.
- I wish she would go away.
- How can I make them understand?

My client Jackie hesitated to tell me about her current life stresses because she thought I would think she was a "terrible and disgusting person." Jackie's elderly mother was widowed, no longer able to drive, and had lost some of her cognitive abilities after suffering a stroke. Jackie was the only one of her siblings who lived near her mother, so she took her grocery shopping every Sunday and called her daily. Jackie told me that after bringing in her groceries, her mother always insisted that she stay "just a little longer" and then made it difficult for her to leave by continually asking Jackie to "please, just do one more thing for me." Jackie's explanations to her mother that she had other errands to run seemed to fall on deaf ears. Her mother complained that Jackie did not spend enough time with her—no matter how late she stayed. Meanwhile, Jackie felt resentment and anger toward her mother and started to dread picking her up every Sunday, anticipating the stressful way the day was going to unfold. She then felt guilty for having such bad feelings about caring for her mother who had made many sacrifices for her over the years.

We decided that this arrangement was not good for Jackie, her mother, or their relationship. Jackie needed to decide how much she could freely give to her mother on Sunday and then set that limit, even if her mother did not understand. Jackie felt instant relief, and eventually, her mother stopped complaining, since she realized that her daughter was going to leave at the designated time regardless of her manipulations. The time they shared became more meaningful and enjoyable for both of them.

Recognizing your individual limits means realizing that your ability to give can vary with differing situations in your life. Perhaps you want to be a person who gives under certain circumstances, but you cannot do it this particular time. Rather than pushing or punishing yourself, try to simply accept your present capacity to give. I know an individual who finds medical settings so anxiety-producing that he rarely visits when his family or friends are in the hospital. Recognizing this restriction on his style of giving, he chooses to call and offer his help after the person is discharged. It is probably better for everyone that he recognizes his limitation and keeps his anxiety out of the hospital room.

An example from my own life shows that self-recognition of even the smallest preferences can turn into a self-nurturing gift. In the morning before work, I cherish my quiet time in which there are no demands on me to interact with people. My husband and I often drive to the office together and stop at the store to buy the daily newspapers. We had established a pattern in which I would be the one to run into the store. When I began feeling more tense during the ride into work, I realized that even that short interaction with people in the store intruded upon my quiet time before work. I am not sure my husband understood my feelings, but he did not mind buying the papers. As small as this gift to myself was, it brought significant peace back to my morning.

Sometimes respecting your limits means larger changes. My client Debbie felt that no matter how hard she tried, she just could not give her best at her job. Although she became involved in more projects that allowed her to use her creativity and she replenished herself on weekends, Debbie continued to find herself bored, restless, and a little depressed. Listening to these signals from her soul, she realized that she spent most of her day working with details and following routine procedures—activities that were inconsistent with her authentic nature. She decided to explore other job possibilities that were more aligned with her strengths and interests.

When your ability to give feels shut down, or your giving feels artificial, this is a signal that you are giving in a way that is not natural to who you are and not good for your soul. You may need to experiment with giving differently, or nurturing yourself before attempting to give in that same way again. Forced giving that is not coming from the heart will only block your true giving potential.

2. Question your giving behaviors that are based on "shoulds."

The second secret of authentic giving is to be aware of the reasons you are giving. Life circumstances, personal situations, and individual desires change, but we often hang on to old habits of giving because we think we "should." Be aware of why you are choosing to give in a particular manner. You do not need to keep giving of yourself in the same way just because you always have done it that way in the past.

For example, my client Marie decorated the office every holiday season, a tradition she started because she wanted to please her boss and co-workers. She enjoyed the projects for the first few years, but now found herself dreading the holidays, primarily because of this extra work. She felt she should continue this activity, however, because she had always done it, and others had come to expect it. When she allowed herself to question this belief, she decided to send out a memo that she was no longer going to be the holiday decorator, but that she would be happy to share her materials with anyone interested in continuing the tradition. By questioning a "should" that kept her busy with unfulfilling activities, Marie gave herself more time to enjoy what would truly give her pleasure.

Likewise, the expectations of others should not be the reason you give. Valued opinions of others may be a considered factor, but only among many—including your authentic beliefs and feelings. My client Maureen needed to challenge the expectations she thought her parents had for her. Maureen was living at her parents' home while she looked for a job after college. Since she had not lived there for the past four years, she was unfamiliar with the household patterns of cleaning. Her parents asked that she "just help around the house" rather than pay rent money. Although she was willing to comply with their request, housecleaning was not one of Maureen's strong suits. Maureen told me that she did not know how much cleaning was expected of her, but she was getting the feeling from her parents that she was not doing enough. Although they never complained directly to her about the amount of housework she did, Maureen thought she was getting "disappointing looks" from them when she was watching television or working at the computer. Whenever she heard them coming down the stairs, she became anxious and would quickly grab a mop, dust cloth, or broom. She felt guilty any time they were cleaning and she was not. Unless she and her parents wanted to work out a more formal contract, we concluded that Maureen must decide the amount of housework she felt was right for her, give that amount of time to cleaning every day, and then stop trying to read her parents' minds.

Finally, question your own expectations for yourself as a giver. Do you want to keep them? Can you accept the personal limits you find that do not live up to your ideals? I frequently tell my clients who do too much, "Just because you *can*, doesn't mean you *should*." In other words, being capable of a giving act does not automatically mean you must do it. For example, perhaps you have the stamina to work with only a few hours sleep, but that does not mean it is the way you should live. I think of my client Mary who filled almost every hour of her week with a task. When asked to do one more thing, she felt she should try to find a way to squeeze it in her already packed schedule rather than turn anyone down.

Give yourself permission to *not* be that ideal giver all of the time. Take care of yourself by sometimes saying "no," even if you want to be the kind of person who usually says "yes." For example, a friend of mine was asked to give a talk at a fund-raising event. Speaking to groups was not easy for her, but she strongly believed in the cause. Acknowledging her true feelings, she offered to mail out flyers rather than give the talk. Perhaps at a later time she might challenge herself, but at this time she chose to enjoy the fund-raising event without the added pressure of a speech.

3. Question your need to please others.

An ancient philosopher once said, "Care about people's approval and you will be their prisoner."[19] When we give because we truly want to, it can never be taken away, whether or not it satisfies others. Even if the receiver does not appreciate the gift, we know that it was given with authentic intentions.

For example, a teenager cleans the house all day in hopes of pleasing her mother. Her mother, however, is preoccupied with other concerns and fails to show the expected gratitude, so her daughter feels unappreciated and regrets the time she spent cleaning. If the daughter had been able to authentically choose to give her time and efforts, then the act itself would be gratifying, and appreciation from her mother would only be an extra gift. If the daughter's *only* reason to clean is to please her mother, she needs to rethink that decision to avoid resentment and depletion.

My client Emily thought that pleasing her husband and trying to become the person she thought he wanted her to be would improve her marriage. As she began to live more according to her authentic nature, she found herself in an unfulfilling marriage and with the need to make some painful decisions about continuing the relationship. It was not until she replaced her need to please with her strength to be herself that she was able to feel and face what was missing in the relationship.

Soulful givers realize that they cannot predict the pleasing of others. Have you ever received a gift that you did not treasure at the time, but later you found it to be invaluable? I am now grateful that my grandparents told me stories about the "old days," but I must admit I did not value these gifts at the time. We all know of works of art and books that were not appreciated until long after the artists and authors had passed on. Your gift may not be valued until a later time and perhaps, not at all. But when given from an authentic heart, its worth endures.

4. Ask for what you need.

The final secret of authentic giving is to ask for what you need rather than expecting someone else to figure it out. As you become more comfortable with your true self, it becomes easier to recognize what you need. For example, perhaps in listening to your desire to spend some time with nature, you decide to take a long weekend in the country. If you prefer to go with a particular friend, don't drop hints, just ask that person to go. If he or she does not want to go, consider a trip alone or asking someone else. Perhaps your preferred traveling partner agrees to go in a few months, but you still feel you need some time away sooner. Allow yourself the chance to find a way to still meet your present needs. Remember, when you ask for something you need, you give others the chance to authentically give to you.

Sometimes sacrifices are part of soulful giving. Go ahead and make the extra effort that your authentic heart is asking of you, but leave the Martyr behind. For example, perhaps you really do not want to give your time at this moment, but you determine that it is necessary. It may be helpful to let someone know that you are stretching yourself and that you are not going to keep doing that extra amount of work. Or you can consider asking for what you need that would make sacrifice less painful.

Mary, a client of mine, saw that it was important to work late every day for a few weeks to help train a new assistant. She let her boss know that she was willing to try to do the extra work for the next six weeks. She wanted to make the sacrifice because she believed that it would benefit many, including herself, in the long run. Honoring her authentic desire, however, did not make her exhausted body feel any better. Considering her needs, she hired her house cleaner to come an extra day a week, and she asked her boss if he would pay for her late dinners out. She also scheduled weekly massages during this intense time period. Although she was stretching her authentic limits, she avoided becoming a Martyr by replenishing herself while giving and asking others to help.

 ## Ten Ways to Practice Giving Authentically

Whether you are nurturing yourself or others, heartfelt gifts are replenishing. When you give according to who you really are, your offerings to others are also gifts of self-expression to yourself. Here are ten ways that you can enhance your authenticity by integrating the *real* you in your everyday giving experiences to yourself and others.

1.   *Recognize and honor your natural way.*
The better you get to know the unique needs and desires of your true nature—body, mind, and soul—the greater your capacity will be to give to others. When you incorporate your natural traits and lifestyle preferences into your gifts, you are giving in harmony with who you are. For example, if you prefer getting up early in the morning rather than staying up late at night and you are going to give a friend some assistance, can you plan to help in the morning rather than in the evening? When you take care of

yourself while taking care of others, the experience is better for everyone.

2.   *Follow your natural inclinations.*

Our desires to give in different situations vary (often for no apparent reason) with our moods. For example, there are moments when we are more inclined toward physical activity and other times when we prefer using our minds. I know for myself that when I am in the mood for mowing the lawn, it is thoroughly enjoyable. When I feel I *have* to do yard work, however, and I would rather be writing, I can feel my energy working against its natural flow. On certain days your social interests may be high, and on other days, you might be struck by your compelling need for solitude. When you consider your true desires at the time, your giving experience will be more pleasurable and invigorating. Many of my clients have found that when they listen to what they "are in the mood for," they often complete tasks at different times than planned, but they still accomplish what they need to and experience more joy in the process.

3.   *Question the giving habits you currently have.*

If you have always done your giving in the same way, consider what parts of it are, and are not, coming from your heart's true desires. What do you want to change? For example, my client Brenda hosts a family picnic every spring. When she stopped and listened to the part of her that was not looking forward to the event, she realized that while she enjoyed most aspects of preparation, she did not like all the yard work that was necessary. She questioned her usual way of doing things and decided she could enhance her enjoyment of the occasion by hiring help to do the yard work. This simple decision resulted in many more years of enjoyable get-togethers for herself and her family members.

4.   Discover what comes easily to you and apply these innate
      traits to your gift-giving acts.

Our natural inclinations are often inherently gifts to others. Just
being *yourself* can be the gift to others. For example, spending
time with dogs and cats is a replenishing gift I give myself that
also happens to nurture animals. Another example of this con-
cept was my father's love for driving. His desire to make car trips
became a welcomed gift to me as he became my "chauffeur" to
many of my booksigning events. He gave me the chance to relax
and see the country while he enjoyed following his natural passion to drive. When you recognize ways in which nurturing
yourself benefits others, you promote the expansion of authentic
giving.

5.   Give in a way that feels right to you, whether it looks right
      or not!

Try giving—or not giving—when you realize that you are engaging in the act simply to appear the proper way to others. Feel the
difference between an authentic desire and giving to meet an expectation of yours or others. For example, go ahead and order
dessert if you want to give yourself a treat, even if nobody else
does. Or give yourself a break from studying when you want to,
even if your friends keep on working.

     If it does not feel right to you to give, even though it seems
to be "the thing to do," *not* giving can be the authentic way for
you to take care of yourself. For example, a friend of mine finds
some of the holidays "too commercial." Although she is very
generous in her giving, she prefers not to give presents for
Mother's Day, Father's Day, or Valentines Day. Likewise, another friend of mine told me that she declined to make a pledge
to a charitable organization supported by all of her co-workers
because it engaged in certain practices she could not support.
Although the easier thing to do would have been to give a dona-

tion, this act of *not* giving was an authentic gift to herself. Furthermore, avoiding this forced giving situation allowed her to choose freely where and when she wanted to donate money.

6.   *Combine your personal interests with gifts to others.*

Most activities we enjoy can be applied to our everyday giving to others. For example, if you want to spend time with your dog and your friend is in need of a listening ear, suggest talking while walking your dog. I remember how my father combined his personal interests with giving time to us as children. On Saturdays, he liked to go to the office in the morning and then run errands in the afternoon. Alternately, each of the four of us would enjoy a special turn alone tagging along with him for the day. I remember looking forward to this unique time where I would get a chance to see my dad as a manager at work and then explore different places after we left the office. His errands could take us anywhere from the dry cleaners and shoe repair shop, to a restaurant for lunch or my grandparents' home. My dad's errands became part of an unfolding adventure and was a wonderful authentic gift—for himself and for us.

7.   *Limit the options you give others to include only those ways that you really want to give.*

Sometimes we feel we must offer more possibilities than we really are comfortable giving, and then we get angry or frustrated when our recipient makes a choice we really did not want them to have. Not only does this take away from our own giving experience, but it also can be confusing for the recipient making an innocent choice. For example, if you really want to do an outside activity on a nice sunny day, don't give your children the choice of a movie. Leave it off the list.

8. *Challenge yourself gently to enhance a weak trait and apply it to a giving situation.*

As you become more aware of your gift-giving abilities, you may also discover nurturing abilities that you want to strengthen. Consider using the choice you make to give as a way to develop a personal trait that is not naturally strong.

My client Valerie had an experience at a wedding reception that illustrates the way we can enhance desired personal traits through giving. She arrived at the reception early, and guests were not yet being allowed in the room. She noticed a physically and mentally disabled woman looking quite distraught over her inability to enter the room. Valerie made the decision to take this woman "under her wing" and talked one of the hotel managers into seating this woman early and relieving her anxiety. Valerie told me she felt good about herself all evening, even though she received no special thank you from the woman or anyone else, since nobody knew what she had done. She told me that she was not comfortable with her general tendency of avoiding people with disabilities, and so in this instance, she challenged herself to an action that did not come naturally to her but required a personal quality she hoped to strengthen. Her gift to this woman proved to be an opportunity for her own personal growth.

9. *Know your values and find ways to incorporate them into your gift-giving.*

You may be surprised to find out all the different ways you can give pleasure to others while expressing and promoting your values. What do you care deeply about? Think of ways you can turn your passion into a gift for others.

I have expressed my values about animal welfare by playing "Dogs and Cats" with my nephews and nieces. Although it began as a spontaneous game, I found it was a way to experientially teach them that animals have feelings, too. Through this creative play, I was able to relay information about general animal care and ways to keep pets safe.

A friend of mine, Molly, is a vegetarian who loves to cook. She takes pleasure in creating vegetarian food dishes for others, but also finds satisfaction in expressing her convictions and promoting the palpability of meatless meals.

10. *Integrate your authentic gifts to avoid burn-out.*

This is especially important for caregivers. When you are in the role of caregiver for a family member or friend with a serious illness or disability, integrating your authentic gifts is even more essential. While this experience can offer a richness to the lives of the caregivers and the recipients, as a caregiver, you need to take the time and effort to become attuned to your own authentic needs and desires and integrate them into your style of care. Listening to your innermost self will increase your capacity to give while expanding your ability to receive the gifts of this experience.

When our family was faced with my father's diagnosis and treatment of esophageal cancer, we quickly learned the importance of considering each person's particular strengths and preferences when dividing caregiving tasks. My mother was elected the medical manager, based on her understanding of procedures and medications. My diplomatic and verbally fluent brother became the spokesman, and my younger brother offered a calming presence and physical strength when needed. My sister's keen awareness of each family member's needs kept each of us at our best, and I was attuned to my father's emotions and sensitivities. When we took "breaks," we also considered the unique ways that each of us replenished. My mother refueled by talking with others and eating in the hospital cafeteria. My sister enjoyed walks. Watching sporting events energized my brothers. I was rejuvenated by petting dogs and cats. With a little creative organizing, we were able to meet my father's needs in ways that were consistent with the unique nature of each of us.

Here are some special tips for soulful caregivers:

Pay attention to your small personal preferences. Carry a bag with favorite items; perhaps a mug for coffee or tea, a good book, pictures, special snacks, or a journal.* Wear comfortable clothes. By taking just a few moments in the morning to consider your own needs in the hours ahead, you can turn potentially depleting tasks into fulfilling experiences.

Consider each person's strengths and preferences when dividing tasks. A stressful caregiving activity for one family member may be second-nature to another. When giving each other time away, make sure each caregiver has the chance to replenish in his or her *own* way.

Be open to the day's unexpected pleasures that may be offered to you. Perhaps you will have the chance to watch a favorite television show, learn something new, read a book, take a nap, or have a special conversation.

Rewards of Authentic Giving

✑ When you give authentically, you not only get to delight in expressing yourself, but others get to know a part of who you really are.

---

* See Appendix C for more information about creating a Giving Bag.

↭ When you give yourself the gift of recognizing your limitations, you develop more understanding for the giving capacity of others.

↭ When you are able to fulfill yourself, you can be more open to receiving what someone else truly has to offer.

↭ When you explore your authentic self, the keys to discovering your greater purpose in life emerges.

↭ When you give authentically, you are helping others listen to their unique selves.

↭ Authentic offerings give back to you because they show you who you are and help you develop the unique aspects of yourself. A client of mine, Maria, gave the gift of patience to her friends. She waited calmly when they were late and listened attentively to their stories as she helped them sort through problems. The ease with which she offered this understanding reaffirmed to her that this was her authentic nature. As she became more aware and proud of this trait, it grew, along with her ability to offer it to others in many more situations.

↭ Authentic giving replenishes your ability to give because it affirms and strengthens your inherent traits that offered the gifts. When my client John wrote songs for his friends, each musical piece validated his identity as a songwriter and enhanced his ability to write more. The more he wrote, the stronger his confidence in his talent became. Each gift of a song replenished his authentic identity, while his musical creations touched many people's lives.

↭ Authentic giving lasts forever. Even though the person, place, or thing to whom you gave may no longer be with you, the affects of the genuine acts of giving go on. For example, if you freely give your time and energy to starting a business that fails to thrive, your gifts are not lost. The knowledge you have acquired and the person you have become remains.

⊷ Authentic giving takes on a life of its own. Teachers have often told me stories about seeing their students many years later and hearing about ways their gifts have impacted students' lives in unexpected ways.

 ## Contemplations for Rediscovering Authentic Giving

⊷ What are some of the natural preferences of your body, mind, and soul? How can you consider your natural body rhythms and lifestyle inclinations when giving to yourself and others?

⊷ List three activities you really enjoy. (If none come readily to mind, think about activities you enjoyed as a child.)

⊷ How can you give yourself a chance to engage in these activities a little more often?

⊷ How can you turn these naturally enjoyable activities into a giving experience for someone else?

⊷ Describe three traits that are a natural part of who you are (things that come easily to you).

⊷ How can you share each trait with others?

⊷ List three traits that do not come easily for you but that you would like to strengthen.

⊷ Can you think of ways that you can develop your desired traits while giving to yourself and to others?

⊷ What beliefs or causes do you feel passionate about?

⊷ Are there ways you can give others the chance to experience these values in the gifts you give them?

LESSON IV
Delight in the Act of Giving

Acting with no expectations,
Leading and not trying to control:
This is the supreme virtue.

*T*he fourth lesson of soulful giving is to let go of the outcome and delight in the giving, itself.

When we can detach from the need to see *results* from our gifts, we become open to the joy in the giving experience itself. The soulful giver is able to be focused in the present, enjoying the process rather than looking to the outcome. Soulful giving asks that we accept the complexities of the human experience and allow life to unfold, rather than attempt to control it. While things may not work out the way we planned or hoped—and the reasons why may remain a mystery—when we can let go of the need for our gifts to produce a specific change, we can experience the true joy of giving.

When we're aiming for a specific result, the "Controller" in us is hard at work, expecting to see measurable changes because of our gift. The Controller wants to improve someone—or themselves—and is constantly trying to make the world better. While these are honorable desires, when our giving focuses solely on the results, the Controller in us is often left feeling inadequate, frustrated, and disillusioned. When things do not work out as planned, the Controller feels a sense of failure.

Most of us have experienced this Controller within us. Take the following Quick Quiz to discover how much the Controller may be affecting your views about giving.

How Does the Controller Affect You?

PART I

YES   NO

____ ____   1. Do you give to yourself only when you believe the gift will improve you?

____ ____   2. Are you more likely to give yourself something if it will enhance your productivity?

____ ____   3. Are you more willing to give yourself a gift if it will improve the image others have of you?

____ ____   4. Do you sometimes refrain from giving yourself a desired gift because it doesn't fit your self-image; in other words, you don't see yourself as being "that kind of person"?

____ ____   5. Are you more likely to give to yourself when this act has produced measurable results in the past?

PART II

YES   NO

____ ____ 6. Do you often give to others expecting it will make them better people?

____ ____ 7. Do you give to others so that they will act the way you want them to?

____ ____ 8. Do you sometimes give to people to enhance the perception they have of you?

____ ____ 9. Do you offer gifts to others to meet the standards you set for yourself as a giver?

____ ____ 10. Have you found yourself giving in a relationship in attempts to get the other person to be more giving to you?

PART III

YES   NO

____ ____ 11. Are many of your gifts designed with the purpose of making positive changes in society?

____ ____ 12. Do you give of yourself to get things accomplished in the world?

____ ____ 13. Do you give to others expecting to see observable differences from your actions?

____ ____ 14. Do you evaluate your gifts to others according to the amount of positive change that has occurred as a result of your gift?

____ ____ 15. Are you often discouraged when you do not see your efforts producing widespread effects?

____ ____ **TOTAL CONTROLLER (C) SCORE**

Score one point for every question you answered "yes." Add all of your points together to obtain your Controller (C) score. Your total score will range from 0 to 15. Your C score shows you to what degree you may knowingly or unknowingly be influenced by the mind set of a Controller in your everyday giving experiences to yourself and others.

Analyzing your Controller Score

0 - 2 points = Joyful Giver
The Controller is seldom present in your giving experience. You are able to give without focusing on the observable results. You enjoy the peace of mind that comes with letting go of the effects of your gifts. You are able to appreciate the complexities of the human experience and accept the unfolding of life's mysteries. You experience the full delight of the experience of giving.

3 - 6 points = Mild Influence
You have experienced some of the peace that comes with letting go of outcome. Some of your giving choices, however, are influenced by a need to control yourself, others, or the world.

7 - 10 points = Under the Influence
It is difficult for you to give to yourself and others unless you see the observable effects of your actions. You tend to blame yourself for not giving in the "right way" or not giving the "right thing" when you do not see the expected results. You may feel bitter about the lack of changes you have seen others and the world make in spite of your efforts. Your attachment to the results of your gifts detracts from the joy and freedom you experience in giving.

11 - 15 points = Controller

You resist accepting your inability to control the vast working of the universe—including many aspects of yourself, others, and the world. Your present satisfaction in giving to yourself and others strongly depends on your ability to see that your gifts result in changes for the better. You may experience daily stress as you try to control anything you can with your actions. You probably feel overloaded with responsibility and often experience a sense of futility when things do not go as expected. You may use acts of giving to manipulate the behavior of others.

Interpreting your Controller Score

Your C score reflects the degree to which the beliefs of a Controller influence your giving style. A high score does *not* mean you have an uncaring or overbearing personality. Rather, a high score reflects the problems inherent in giving that is attached to controlling an outcome.

Analyzing Your Subscale Score

To understand more fully how the Controller in you is affecting your giving, take a few more minutes to look at three areas that may be blocking you from joyful giving.

Give yourself one point for every "yes" in PART I.
This is your <u>Self-Critic</u> score.

Give yourself one point for every "yes" in PART II.
This is your <u>Proven Helper</u> score.

Give yourself one point for every "yes" in PART III.
This is your <u>World Changer</u> score.

For each subscale, your score will range from 0 - 5. Take special note of the subscales where you have the highest score. These represent the greatest obstacles between you and giving in the spirit of appreciation.

0 points = No interference
This obstacle is not interfering with soulful giving.

1 to 2 points = Some interference
You may have some behavior and thoughts of this obstacle that keep you from joyful giving.

3 to 5 points = Interference
You are aware of the effects of this obstacle when giving to others and when neglecting yourself. It is important to pay extra attention to questioning the beliefs that go along with this obstacle so that you can rediscover the joy of giving.

 Three Obstacles to Joyful Giving

Let's look at each of the obstacles that maintain the Controller in your giving experiences.

1. The "Self-Critic" Obstacle

The first obstacle to joyful giving is making judgments before and after giving to yourself. Self-Critics will consider nurturing themselves *only* when it will make them better people, increase their accomplishments, or improve their images. They deny gifts to themselves when the gifts are inconsistent with their view of their "ideal" selves.

How often do you give to yourself because it will be "good for you?" Perhaps you buy yourself a book that will improve your time management or a calculator that will help you balance bills more quickly and accurately. Or you give yourself a gift you believe will increase your capacity to give more to others. For example, a busy mother may allow herself the time and money to take a ceramic class only because she intends to teach this art to her children. An individual may give himself an expensive new suit only because it enhances his professional appearance in the business world. A busy office manager told me that she takes a week every year relaxing by the ocean, but she does it because she expects this vacation to increase her physical stamina and mental efficiency once she returns to work.

The Self-Critic in us may also deny gifts that are inconsistent with our self-image. For example, my client Molly was reluctant to buy a van because she had always considered vans to be "decadent and unnecessarily big." While she saw the advantages to this vehicle in transporting her four children and a dog, she told me she was afraid her friends would think that her change of heart reflected "a loss of my social values to the self-indulgences of suburbia." Another client told me that she secretly enjoys massages, facials, and pedicures, but does not want others to know that she spends money on these "self-indulgences."

2. The "Proven Helper" Obstacle

The second obstacle to joyful giving is needing your gifts to improve or change someone else—in the way *you* think is best for them. My client Nancy, for example, bought her partner an exercise machine that he never uses. Furthermore, what she regarded as a thoughtful and caring act was seen by her partner as "a daily nagging reminder." I also hear parents complain that their children do not play with toys they bought them to help develop certain skills. I once counseled disappointed parents who had invested money in refinishing the basement of their house expecting that it would keep their wandering teenagers home at night.

The Proven Helper, motivated by the desire to control another person's behavior, appears frequently in our intimate relationships. We assume that our acts of giving will produce certain changes for the better in the person with whom we are involved. For example, we might expect our partner to utilize the closet organizer or a read the book on practical ways to save money. My client Sheila buys her "ungrateful" husband new pants and shirts every year before the holidays, only to feel disappointed and angry as he continues to wear his torn and tattered jeans to family gatherings. Teachers often express feeling inadequate when they are unable to see their students advancing from the lessons they are trying to give to them. Therapists may become dissatisfied with their work and themselves when their patients do not make the changes that the therapists thought would be best. Disguised as acts of giving, we often want to "help others" change a behavior in a direction that will benefit us, and we are frustrated when the receiver does not go along with our plan.

Trying to change someone can be very frustrating, as my client Millie reported to me. She was upset that her husband was staying out late with the guys on Friday nights, and she tried many different strategies of giving, all with the intent of squelching his desire for these late night escapades. First, she tried cooking his favorite dinners, dressing in her sexiest clothes, and offering him a back massage and full control of the television remote control. When he still chose to stay out late with the guys after all her efforts, Millie reported feeling "like a sucker." She regretted her acts of giving and felt more angry and frustrated. She then decided to try holding back her usual gifts of dinner and pleasant conversation, but this act also failed to alter his behavior. Even when she decided to try the strategy of not being home at all on Friday nights, it made no difference in his actions—and she was uncomfortable with her own behavior. Millie concluded that she wanted to stay in the relationship, but that she needed to decide what she truly wanted to give of herself to her husband at this time, regardless of his actions. She found enjoyable ways to spend her Friday evenings, both alone and with friends, as she let go of trying to change him through her acts of giving and not giving.

Both givers and receivers are uncomfortable when a gift is given with the expectation of controlling an outcome. The giver is disappointed and often blames herself for not giving quite the right way to get the change she wanted. The receiver feels obliged to respond in the way that is expected. While our persistent efforts to change may mean well, this pressure to improve someone can actually stifle the ability of others to express their own true selves.

Sometimes the Proven Helper wants to demonstrate to those observing that they are helpful people. Think about it: Why do you give to the person ringing the bell outside of the store or holding the can in the street? Are you concerned what others may think of you if you don't? Is it truly your choice to give to the organization represented by that individual? Or is the Proven Helper in you hard at work to "look good" in the eyes of others?

3. The "World Changer" Obstacle

It is certainly an honorable desire to want to make the world a better place. However, when our goal for giving is to improve things on a large scale where change is beyond our control, we set ourselves up to feel like a failure.

The World Changer may appear to offer advice freely but is satisfied only when the advice is taken. For example, my client

Hayley described herself as a failure when a free lecture she gave on recycling did not increase her community's participation in the project.

Life events that are transient, uncontrollable, and unpredictable frustrate the World Changer. Someone might give their all to a politician that changes his position once elected. Another giver may spend endless hours trying to get a referendum passed that fails. Some may go through a lot of trouble to affect a situation that, unbeknownst to them, is destined to follow its own course. How about the individual whose relentless efforts result in a ruling that is overturned later? I remember a story about a community that rallied to save an old oak tree from being cut down for a new development. Through the efforts of many, the tree was saved, but within a few months it was struck down by lightning. I wonder if the people who gave to this cause felt that their gift was worthless.

The problem is not in the intent of the gift or in the changing circumstances. The problem is that the World Changer's joy in giving *depends* on a particular outcome, and they often feel inadequate and disillusioned when something different unfolds.

 Four Secrets
of Joyful Giving

The key to joyful giving is appreciation. Appreciating the complexities of the human experience. Opening to life's mysteries. Allowing events to unfold. Once we embrace appreciation, we are no longer limited by our own visions or goals. Giving with the spirit of appreciation allows the intrinsic joys and pleasant surprises of the present act of giving to flow.

1. Give to yourself without judgment.

The first secret to giving joyfully is to allow yourself to suspend "logical" assessment so you can hear and appreciate the deepest needs of your soul. The soulful giver considers the whole person and embraces self-nurturance without judgment.

Perhaps you find enjoyment in taking a clock apart, even if you are unable to fix it. You may want to take an interesting class even though it doesn't count toward your major or get you a better job. Spend a day, or part of a day, doing things in a manner that appeals to you but may not be "logical" or produce "results." Eat dessert first. Do the fun activity before your work is done. You don't have to finish one project that you enjoy before you can start another one that is appealing to your mood right now. Sometimes we need to trust that our intuition knows what we need—whether it is an illogical order to our day or a gooey chocolate dessert.

2. Give without looking for proof that you have helped.

The second secret of joyful giving is to let go of trying to make somebody a better person. When we stop looking for proof that our gift has helped, we can more easily accept others for who they are. We also put the responsibility for change back in the individual's hands, letting them know we believe they are in control of their lives. They are free to use our unconditional gifts any way that they want, or do not want, to use them.

Question your motives for wanting to give something to help someone. Are you hoping they will change? Do you still want to give your help if it will *not* change their behavior? I was once told this heart-warming story that illustrates the delight of giving truly detached from the outcome. A wealthy restaurant owner gave a waitress a substantial amount of money because she told him that her child had a life-threatening condition and needed an operation. After he gave her the money, the waitress quit. The generous owner was later told that the child did not have the life-threatening condition and never needed the costly surgery. Having no regrets about his decision to help, the owner's only remark was that he was glad that the child was healthy and spared the operation.

3. Let go of your pre-conceived notions of what a helper should be.

Whose standards do you follow for being a caring and helping person? The third secret to delighting in your giving is to allow flexibility in your giving, letting go of some pre-determined agenda and taking your needs into account. Perhaps you feel in need of a break from helping others, a break from "always being there," a vacation from your busy schedule—but you are afraid of what others might think about your "lesser" degree of helping. Are you afraid others will not think you are a good worker or caring mother if you slow down the pace? Do *you* believe you can be a good worker or a caring mother if you slow down the pace? As you experience the natural flow of giving to and from your soul, you will see that the ways in which you can help may fluctuate from day to day and will vary according to your own needs. Let the soulful helper replace your old ideas of what a helper should be.

4. Allow life to unfold.

The fourth secret of joyful giving is to allow your place in the world to unfold rather than trying to change the world. In eastern philosophy, there is a wise caution about our need to change the world:

> The universe is sacred, You cannot improve it.
> If you try to change it, you will ruin it.
> If you try to hold it, you will lose it.[20]

In his book *Callings: Finding and Following an Authentic Life*, Gregg Levoy also discusses the necessity of letting go of outcome:

> Every sacrifice . . . every step toward action, every response to a call necessitates a leap of faith and is done without knowing the outcome.[21]

When we decide to give with this "leap of faith," rather than with the expectation of controlling some aspect of the world, we are free to more fully see and explore the beauty and complexity in the mysterious workings of the universe. Mary's story illustrates this "leap of faith" giving. Mary chooses to give to the environment by recycling paper products, cans, and bottles every week. This program is new to her community and few participate in it. Some of Mary's neighbors have told her that the items she painstakingly washes and separates end up mixed with the garbage. Although Mary does not know if her efforts are producing the desired outcome, her beliefs motivate her to continue to recycle. She feels good about doing her part and lets go of the results of her actions.

Sometimes painful moments occur as we recognize our inability to control situations. This may help us to uncover possibilities we never before considered. Sometimes a negative result from our giving provides an opportunity to learn. For the soulful giver the outcome cannot take away the original delight in the act of giving.

People who are in the role of caregiver of a loved one with a serious illness or disability quickly discover the need to give joyfully without expectation. Even with our offering the best care possible, our loved ones may succumb to the disease or not improve. They may get better for a little while, and then get worse. They may suffer. Perhaps they feel depressed and lonely in spite of all of our efforts. Most of the time, there are no "quick fixes," and as caregivers we realize that day-to-day life is going to be drastically different. The more we can accept the elements of the situation that are not in our control, the more we will be open to the unfolding of this unknown experience and its offerings. Our efforts may not result in a cure, but we can have peace of mind knowing that our gifts of care are worthy in and of themselves, everyday.

Ten Ways to Practice Joyful Giving

1.   Re-frame your reason for giving.
When you realize that your motivation for a gift is to get a certain result, explore more satisfying reasons to give. Label the desired results your personal hopes or dreams, but not the basis for your offerings. It is important to recognize the difference between your *hope* for an outcome and your *need* for results to justify your act of giving. You may, for example, give to a child who does not show any appreciation, but that does not have to diminish your loving reasons for giving. Honor your beliefs and feelings, even when your acts of giving do not produce the changes you had desired.

2.   Be aware of what detracts from your joy in giving.
Pay attention to what interferes with the pleasure of your gift, whether it is to yourself or to someone else. My client Jane, for example, planned a vacation with an all-inclusive package at a specific resort. While she enjoyed many aspects of the vacation, she felt confined by the pre-planned schedules and realized she would have preferred the chance for more independent exploration and varied eating experiences. This discovery of her pref-

erences was invaluable in planning an excursion that would better suit her true desires the following year.

I experienced the value of this lesson first-hand while practicing a random act of kindness to a stranger on an airplane. I offered my aisle seat to the passenger sitting in the middle seat next to me. While I enjoyed this person's surprised delight as we traded seats, my enjoyment of the flight quickly diminished as I became claustrophobic and felt squished. My arms and legs developed cramps. My good intentions resulted in great discomfort that stayed with me even after arriving at my destination. I learned that when I am giving just for the fun of it, I need to find ways that are fun for both the giver and me.

3.   *Explore your self-nurturing options before choosing one.*
When you are going to give yourself a break, a treat, or something just for you, think about what you *really* want. Mindless television watching and channel-surfing are examples of gifts to ourselves that we don't really choose. Many of my clients have told me that although they come home from work exhausted, they plan on "getting some work done" before going to bed. They turn on the television set "for just a minute" before starting their tasks and find themselves staring at the picture, changing channels, and watching programs that do not even interest them. Rather than selecting a replenishing activity, they passively stare at the television screen and miss the chance to nurture themselves with a program they would enjoy or another form of relaxation that truly appeals to them.

Perhaps you are in the habit of giving to yourself in a certain way, but there might be another kind of self-nurturing you would find more satisfying. For example, my client Vince went out to lunch every day with his coworkers until he questioned this action and discovered that it was a draining, not replenishing, experience. His lunch hour felt like a continuation of his work as a consultant. He had developed this habit without considering his options or his need for some time to himself during lunch. Vince decided to have lunch with his coworkers once a week and chose to spend the other lunch hours alone.

When I have days in the office with appointments scheduled in the morning and late into the evening, I will often go home for a few hours in the middle of the day. I have found that this time away is most replenishing when I nurture *all* of me—body, mind, and soul. I get out of my work clothes, play my favorite music, simmer some aromatic potpourri, and then sit and decide what I would most like to do with this time. I might choose to play with my dogs, take a walk, enjoy a nap, or eat my favorite foods. I may sip a cup of tea while sitting in my backyard. Not only do I experience more pleasure in my reprieve at home, I find myself more inclined to enjoy the time spent back at the office.

4.   *Add the little extra touches to simple pleasures and small comforts.*

When you decide to give yourself a nurturing gift, consider ways that you can make the experience even a little more enjoyable. Involve as many senses as possible: add pleasing aromas, tastes, textures, colors, or sounds whenever you can.

Whenever you can, ask yourself, "What else can I add to this experience to make it more fulfilling?" If, for example, you are having a delicious dessert, put it on a pretty plate, savor each bite, add a cherry on top, and leave off the guilt. Or if you decide to take a nap in the middle of the day, lift any restrictions you usually have on the length of time. Enjoy waking up when your body feels naturally rejuvenated.

5.   *Give yourself a gift that you desire even when you cannot readily see its value.*

Sometimes you need to trust your intuitive wisdom and nurture yourself for "no good reason." Give yourself something that you don't really "need." Indulge in something extravagant or unnecessary, but desired and pleasurable. Read a mystery, have a present to yourself gift-wrapped, or lounge in bed "just for the fun of it" when you are not even tired.

I think of a friend of mine who fell in love with a stuffed teddy bear we discovered in a toy store. Although initially reluctant to buy it, she grasped it in her arms and with child-like excitement, smiled and giggled all the way to the cash register. My friend and I often look back fondly on this particular shopping expedition.

6.   *Find the gifts in situations that you cannot readily change or control.*

When you find yourself in an unexpected situation that is asking you to give more than you had originally planned, add a little self-nurturing to the experience to enhance the joy. For example, if you are on your way to help someone and find yourself stuck in traffic, take the opportunity to listen to a favorite tape or try a new radio program. Enjoy the extra long break away from your routine. Sing. Relax. Enjoy the sights. Let go of your ability to affect the situation and enjoy the pleasures that are right there. The replenishment you give yourself during this unexpected delay will further enhance the joy you find when you finally do reach your destination.

Look for small joys in unwelcomed situations by changing your focus. For example, if you have agreed to attend a party that holds no interest for you, think about ways you might still enjoy yourself. Are you a people watcher? Or perhaps you could engage others in conversation about a cause that is important to you. You might enjoy playing with the pets or children present, or getting some new decorating ideas. Or focus on the adventure of tasting new foods. Be on the alert for the gifts "behind the scene."

7. *Let a difficult problem remain unresolved for a while.*

Let yourself "stay stuck." Let answers unfold in their own time. When you let go of coming up with your own answer, you are making room for giving experiences to surprise you and to offer creative solutions to blocked problems.

My client Leah embraced the gift of being stuck after the hard disk on her computer crashed. She worked for hours to no avail. While she was still struggling to save multiple files of work, a good friend called and asked if she would come over and help her daughter who was having difficulty preparing for an important algebra test the following day. Although Leah wanted to help, she felt she needed to focus on her own computer crisis. Empathizing with her friend's daughter's frustration, however, Leah decided to leave her problem for a while and try her hand at algebra. While she shared her mathematical knowledge, her friend's brother, a computer expert, happened to stop by and offered to help Leah with her computer problem that same evening. He solved it in just a few minutes, saving her countless hours of work and aggravation. She had no intention of trading her tutorial skills for computer expertise—but that is what naturally unfolded when Leah allowed herself to stay stuck and chose to help someone else.

Another client has a different way to make room for the surprising way that gifts can appear. When she finds herself in a trying situation or bogged down with worries that seem to have no solution, she lets go of her perceived control over the problem and "gives it to the angels." Giving away this control invites the mysterious workings of the universe to present its gifts.

8. *Don't let disappointing results take the gift away from you.*
My friend Allison is a vegan (she doesn't eat meat or dairy products), and she enjoys baking nontraditional treats that surprise others with how tasty they can be. For Thanksgiving, she baked a non-dairy pumpkin pie, but it was not well-received by her family. Allison, however, enjoyed finding the recipe, going to the health food store to get the ingredients, baking it, and having a piece herself. In spite of the pie's failure to please her family's tastes that evening, Allison had the pleasure of preparing the pie, and she got the chance to reaffirm her own beliefs. She plans to continue expressing her values by bringing these kinds of goodies for her family to try and for herself to enjoy—whether or not her delicacies are appreciated in the way she had hoped.

9. *Imagine that your gift might never be used by the recipient, and let it go.*
I often hear people's disappointment when they discover that something they had given a friend or relative was stuffed in a closet or given away. Allow the act of giving to be valuable in and of itself. Forget the idea that your gift's value lies in the recipient's usage of it. Perhaps the gift you give will get passed on to someone else. I personally enjoy receiving a book I already own so that I can pass it on. The value of unused gifts is wonderfully portrayed in Mitch Album's book *Tuesdays with Morrie*, where he relates that the favorite foods of his dying friend, Morrie, continued to be brought over by friends and relatives, even when Morrie was too sick to eat them. The foods served as symbolic gifts of love and nurturance.

10.   *Recognize that the fruits of your gifts may not be observed in your lifetime.*

Remember that you never really know the full and long-term impact of your gifts. Frank Capra's classic movie, *It's a Wonderful Life*, illustrates the multiple ways that soulful gifts influence others and change the course of the world—sometimes in ways we could never imagine. In this uplifting story, an angel shows a disheartened man, George Bailey, who is on the brink of suicide, the multiple ways he has helped the lives of many by just being himself throughout his life. Let the results of your giving unfold in their own time. Accept the mystery of not knowing the full impact of your efforts.

 *Rewards of Joyful Giving*

↩ The experience of giving is full of intrinsic pleasures.

↩ When you give for the pleasure of giving, not for the purpose of controlling, your joy is not dependent on others.

↩ When you let go of preconceived results, you will be open to discovering new possibilities.

↩ When you stop setting yourself up for self-blame, you become less blaming of others.

↩ As you let go of outcome, you are more able to accept the true self you find.

↩ When you detach from the outcome, you will experience the peace that comes with faith in a greater purpose beyond yourself.

❧ When you are not expecting others to behave in certain ways, you are more easily able to accept them as they are, allowing the natural pleasures of authentic relationships to bloom.

❧ The act of giving in and of itself will surprise you with its many pleasures.

❧ Joy from the giving experience itself is never lost and cannot be taken away.

❧ Giving from the heart never loses its value.

❧ Open to possibilities, the soul can turn a dull moment into a nurturing gift.

Contemplations
for Rediscovering Joyful Giving

❧ What are some ways that you give to yourself expecting a positive change? Do you struggle with not living up to your own standards for self-improvement? What would it be like to stop expecting yourself to change but still freely give yourself soul-nourishing gifts and experiences?

❧ Do you maintain some daily helping behavior because you are expecting somebody to change? What would it be like to give up that need for them to change and just accept the persons as they are? If they do not change, what can you change about yourself that will make it easier to accept them?

❧ Think back on a time when you gave and gave and did not get the results for which you had hoped. Can you look at those acts of giving now through more soulful eyes and see the rewards that were present in the experience itself?

❧ What have been some of your most enjoyable giving experiences? What elements added to the pleasure?

❧ Think of a way that you would like to give "just for the fun of it."

❧ What kind of giving experience ignites your passions?

Experience the Expanding Capacity to Give

The Master doesn't seek fulfillment,
Not seeking, not expecting,
She is present and can welcome all things.

*T*he fifth lesson of soulful giving is to let each giving experience expand your capacity to give.

There is a wonderful, surprising result of giving to your heart's content without giving yourself away. When you align your actions with your innermost desires, you not only increase your pleasure in giving, but also your capacity to give.

When your gifts are not motivated by a need for recognition, rewards, or results, you will find deeper meaning in the everyday acts of giving. This, in turn, will increase your desire to find more ways to give. The elements of soulful giving are self-perpetuating. Each one creates a cycle that maintains itself.

The Cycle of Unconditional Giving

1. Accepting what is, you give.
2. Your act of giving strengthens your commitment to acceptance.
3. Being more accepting, you are naturally able to give more.
4. Giving continues to expand your capacity for acceptance.

The Cycle of Authentic Giving

1. Recognizing your individuality, you give from your unique traits.
2. Your act of giving reaffirms and strengthens your uniqueness.
3. This affirmation replenishes your true self, and you are naturally able to give more.
4. Giving continues to expand your capacity to live authentically.

The Cycle of Joyful Giving

1. Appreciating the complexities of life and letting go of control, you give.
2. Your act of giving strengthens your commitment to appreciation.
3. With an expanded ability to appreciate, you naturally give more.
4. Giving continues to expand your capacity for appreciating the journey of life.

Four Secrets
of Expanded Giving

While the expansion of your capacity to give is a natural out-growth of soulful giving, the following ideas can help you more easily tap into this life-enriching process.

1. Make the choice.

Choose to give to others by listening to your heart. It is important to remember that the decision to give to others is *your* choice. Sometimes it may feel as though you have no other option but to give, but ultimately you are still making a choice. Recognizing that every decision to give is *yours* enhances the experience right from the start.

Sometimes your choice may require extra effort and energy. Soulful givers learn to give themselves extra rest and care before embarking on a demanding task. Don't wait until your body forces you to take action! Falling asleep at the table while you are trying to complete a project only results in a stiff neck and the uneasy feeling of interrupted sleep, whereas making the choice to give yourself a nap in a comfortable place will replenish your ability to enjoy and complete your work a little later.

When you choose to give even though it is a hardship for you, leave the Martyr behind by recognizing your unique ability to extend yourself under these circumstances. Appreciate your personal strengths that make it possible for you to go the extra mile. Take pride and pleasure in that part of you that is choosing to give. Consider the way that your individual sacrifice may contribute to the greater good.

Choose to give to yourself. Remember: Self-nurturing can expand your capacity to give to others *only* when you choose to take the full pleasure offered and leave the guilt behind! Don't cheat yourself out of a fully replenishing weekend by starting to anticipate the work week ahead. If you are giving yourself the gift of a walk in nature, don't stay preoccupied with all the work you should be doing, or you will miss the experience's full potential to renew you. Fuel your giver within with premium gas! Stop and think how you would *really* like to spend your gift of time to yourself. When you recognize that self-nurturing expands your ability to give to others, it might be easier to decide to give to yourself freely and without guilt.

Choose when NOT to give. Sometime it is important to make the decision not to give to others. Perhaps you are feeling too depleted to consider the favor that is being asked of you. Paradoxically, a decision to *not* give at this time can increase your capacity to give. To fully experience this gift of sometimes *not* giving, you need to accept your limitations and your inability to give all of the time. Do not take away from the experience by second-guessing yourself, feeling guilty, or regretting the decision. Make the choice and then allow the full affects of this action— including a stronger desire and an increased capacity to give in a different way or at another time.

2. Embrace the experience wholeheartedly.

When you decide you are going to give, then wholeheartedly engage yourself in all aspects of the experience. Choose it, then do it! Be like the gardener who has decided to plant seeds. Rather than focusing on whether or not the flowers will grow, the gardener fully engages in the act of planting, taking in the complete experience: feeling the soil, digging with energy, sensing the sun, getting dirty, and enjoying the satisfaction of sowing the seeds.

When you decide to give, give—and receive—the most you can by being fully there. Let go of any ideas you have about pleasing others, keeping things equal, or effecting a change. These thoughts take away from you and your recipient's ability to fully experience the giving. Focus on the immediate sensations. Let the joy of giving completely contribute to your desire to seek out similar experiences again.

For example, if you decide to give your partner a break and let him be sloppy, then *really* give him the gift. Do not nag even once. If you are going to sacrifice your convenience for the day by letting your daughter have the car, then give her that present without adding comments that are meant to elicit guilt or detract from her joy. Once you have made your choice, let the recipient of your gift feel that your whole heart is in the act! To expand the giving heart, let the experience be the best it can be for both you and the receiver.

Choose for the moment, not forever. When you decide to give, remember that this is a choice you are making only for *right now*. Embracing the moment now does not lock you into a lifetime pattern of this kind of action. Sometimes the heart can stretch its ability to give and keep on giving, but other times, it needs to stop and regenerate to expand its capacity at its own pace. You can choose to respond differently the next time you are presented with similar circumstances. But go with what you have embraced for now.

3. *Respond to your soul's desire to give.*

Listen to the urge in your heart and follow it. Let a new opportunity to give interfere with your plans. Decide to stretch your limits—but remember to give yourself the added replenishment to make it all happen. When you are not sure, go ahead and take the chance and let your heart take the "leap of faith" into giving. If a story touches your heart and compels you to give, don't hesitate.

And when an impulsive act of giving leads you to a situation that feels beyond your capacity, try and make the stretch. Your capacity to give can grow when needed. Allow one giving experience to lead you to another.

The soul's desire to give is never more evident than when we are deeply moved by catastrophic or tragic events that affect a large group of people. Like water rushing through the floodgates of a dam, we rise as a compassionate people with an outpouring of giving that cannot be stopped. When tragedy strikes a group, a community, or the world, the power of soulful giving can make the toughest days more bearable.

Our gifts of money for those less fortunate, a helping hand for those who have fallen, or a strong shoulder for a friend in need of support are all gifts from the heart that offer comfort, peace, and a shared bond of concern. When we come together as diverse people with the shared desire to give, we bring the glimmer of hope that a devastating tragedy will not demolish the human spirit.

4. Like the banyan tree, let your heart grow as it keeps on giving.

The banyan tree is a wonderful example of the expansive cycle of giving. This unique fig tree continually gives, and it continually benefits from giving. The more it gives, the stronger it becomes. As the single-trunk banyan tree nourishes itself, it produces aerial roots that, in turn, bury themselves into the ground. When nourished, these branches form the trunks of new trees. These new trunks not only provide additional support for the original tree, but each trunk becomes its own tree, producing *more* aerial roots that later become trunks and create more new trees. I think you get the picture: The more the banyan tree gives, the stronger it becomes, and the greater its capacity to give and grow.

Native to India, banyans are rare in the United States. In the 1870s, one was planted in Maui as a gift from the Lahaina Smith family. Now described as a mini-forest, this tree originally planted as a single trunk stands over fifty feet high and covers over an acre of land. In 1925 another banyan was planted in Florida as a gift to Thomas Edison. Once only four feet tall, this tree now covers more than four hundred square feet—and it's still growing!

The banyan tree's expanding capacity to give is indisputable. Take it to heart: soulful giving is a process that grows . . . taking on life of its own.

 ## *My Giving Journey*

For a year-and-a-half, I was privileged to embark on a life-changing journey as I accompanied my father through months of living with an aggressive cancer. I have probably never given so much to one person in one time period—and I definitely have never received so many gifts at the same time!

Although I had started this book before my father's diagnosis, I believe it is more than coincidence that my writing about giving took place during this time. I had a chance to experience firsthand the wondrous ways that soul-centered giving expands our capacity to give. I discovered gifts within me that affirmed my deepest self. As I gave, I was given abundant gifts that enriched my everyday life. And I was so moved by the responses to my gifts that I was inspired to give more.

As I close this book, perhaps if I share with you my experience of the "three A's" of soulful giving—Acceptance, Authenticity, and Appreciation—you will catch a glimmer of deep rewards of soulful giving for yourself, for those you love, and for our troubled world.

Giving with Authenticity

I began this journey by listening to my authentic nature as a helper and caretaker. I knew I wanted to participate in all aspects of my father's illness: diagnostic testing, surgeries, chemotherapy, radiation, and countless meetings with doctors, nurses, lab technicians, researchers, and later, hospice workers. By listening to my heart's desire to be present in every phase, I discovered inner strengths that I never knew I had: staying calm in emergencies, offering emotional support to my father, becoming comfortable with hospitals, speaking up, slowing down, facing fear, and finding courage.

As the challenges ahead of us intensified, unexpected gifts to my soul strengthened my ability to give from a deeper place. My dad and I had many new opportunities to talk, and our humorous, tender, and thought-provoking conversations formed an even closer bond between the two of us.

Throughout this experience, it seemed only natural to nurture myself with good food, rest, nature walks, inspiring books, and comfortable clothes. When I needed to spend numerous hours waiting for my father, or staying with him while he slept, I began carrying with me a "giving bag"—a tote bag filled with special soul-nourishing items, such as a favorite fruit and candy, a sketch pad, a book of poems, and soothing lotions. By taking care of my unique needs, these gifts to myself refueled my soul's ability to keep on giving.

Giving with Acceptance

Of course, I would rather that my Dad was cancer-free and healthy. But it was only as I could begin to accept this "unfairness" of life that I could be open to the gifts that the new situation had to offer.

Acceptance included honoring the full range of my emotions—anger, fear, sadness, worry, hope that he'd be okay . . . the whole gamut. Acceptance meant recognizing that I would have to sacrifice considerable time with my husband, my pets, and my work . . . just about every aspect of my everyday life as I knew it. It also meant choosing to embrace each phase of my dad's treatment with no expectation of a specific or fair outcome.

Acceptance gave me a new ability to view each day as a gift, regardless of what it brought. I no longer avoided the more difficult aspects that I would otherwise have viewed as unrewarding. Acceptance increased my desire to more fully participate in this all-encompassing journey.

Giving with Appreciation

When I was forced to accept that this unique journey of the soul with my father was coming to an end, I found myself letting go of the need to understand "why" or to predict the final steps of his courageous trek. Embracing the spirit of appreciation and building on my expanding capacity to give in new ways, I tried to take in the many mysteries of this final stage of earthly life and become open to each day's offerings.

Influenced by my father's remarkable attitude, I found new joy in life's simple pleasures: watching squirrels scurrying in the trees or delighting in a sunny blue sky. The phrase *"living in the moment"* took on new significance for me. I developed an appreciation for many of the things I had previously taken for granted, such as the ability to get around easily, waking up with energy, and having a healthy appetite.

One of the many gifts of appreciation I received was a deeper understanding and admiration of individuals living with life-threatening illnesses—and those who care for them. I also experienced a closer connection with each member of my family, a more fervent faith in the greater purpose of each of our lives, and a stronger belief in an eternal bond that connects all of us.

The final gift of this journey came in the wee hours of a dark night. My authentic desires to be with my Dad to the end, along with an ability to give in ways I was never able to give before, enabled me to be present during my dad's last hours of life on earth. I received an extraordinary gift of hope: At the moment my Dad passed away, I saw him surrounded by light, and I was filled with an immense sense of peace and calm.

As my role as giver to my father ends, I cannot deny the sadness and setbacks along the way, but they are small compared to the meaning and joy of this gift-filled, soulful journey with him. I miss my father immensely—he held a special place in my heart.

But amidst the sorrow of my soul is a heart overflowing with a greater desire to give than ever before. This giving journey with my father had a profound affect on expanding my soul's capacity to give.

 Rewards of Expanded Giving

Your journey will take you to different places than mine, and your challenges may teach you different lessons. But this I do know: The infinite rewards of this whole unfolding, soul-filled process of giving await you.

- ⬵ When you expand your giving, you enhance the soulfulness of your daily life and the lives of others.

- ⬵ As you free yourself from the limits and restrictions of half-hearted giving, your soul will thrive as your capacity to give expands.

⋄ The potential of your giving experiences is unlimited. Each time you give, giving expands in the world.

⋄ As your giving grows, you will experience the deeper mystery, enjoyment, and celebration of the whole of life.

⋄ Like the banyan tree, the more you give, the more you benefit from giving. And the larger your giving capacity grows, the more you will have to give.

⋄ The desire to give can overpower the fear of the unknown.

⋄ Expanded giving in your relationships means expanded meaning in your life.

⋄ A fulfilled soul can't resist giving. Acts of giving fulfill the soul.

Contemplations for Expanded Giving

⋄ Think about a time when you gave of yourself and it enabled you to give in an even stronger way the next time you were in a similar situation.

⋄ Think of a time when you were asked to give in ways that you did not know that you could, but you went ahead and took the leap. What was that experience like for you? What gifts did it give you?

⋄ Can you remember a time when you were in the flow of a giving experience, paying no attention to time and feeling as though you had unlimited energy? How did you feel?

⋄ What kinds of giving situations give you the most joy?

❧ Think about some of the most meaningful and joyful life experiences you have had. Can you see how giving played a role in them?

❧ As you expand your capacity to give, what does your soul need for replenishment?

APPENDICES

APPENDIX A
Suggestions for Discussion Groups

Format:
A Five Week Course
1 to 1 ½ hours per session.
The time can easily be shortened or lengthened
by varying the number of activities or discussion questions.

WEEK I.   *Giving from your Heart*

OPENING EXERCISE

✦ Offer ways for people to meet each other.

OPENING DISCUSSION QUESTIONS

✦ Depending on the size of your group, discuss these questions as one group, or break up into small groups of 2-4 people:

- How do you experience giving in your life?
- How is your energy level? Do you feel drained and exhausted by the demands of life or do you feel fairly comfortable with the balance in your life?
- What is your most recent experience of saying "yes" when you really wanted to say "no"?

ACTIVITY

✦ Have participants take the self-inventory "Do You Need Gifts from Yourself?"on pages 31-32 and score it.

✦ Let the results open up the following discussion questions:

- What did you discover about yourself?
- How hard, or easy, is it for you to give to yourself?
- What interferes or helps?

ASSIGNMENT FOR NEXT WEEK

- Read the *Introduction* and *Lesson I: Give Wholly to Yourself.*
- Choose one of the "Ten Simple Ways To Practice Giving to Yourself" (see pages 34-37) this week. Take note of your feelings about the experience for discussion next week.

WEEK II. *Giving Unconditionally*

OPENING DISCUSSION QUESTIONS

⮕ Depending on the size of your group, discuss these questions as one group, or break up into small groups of 2-4 people:

- How did you choose to nurture yourself this week?
- How did it affect your ability to give to others?
- In your reading on giving wholly to yourself, what seemed especially important to you?

ACTIVITY

⮕ Have everyone take the Quick Quiz "How Does the Trader Affect You?" on pages 40-41 and score it. Discuss the interpretation of the results.

⮕ Discuss these questions (as one group or in smaller groups):

- Have you ever been in a situation where you felt you gave more than your fair share?
- Have you ever been in a situation where you did not get back what you expected?

⮕ Present the idea of *acceptance* as a way to decrease the influence of the Trader (see pages 19, 50-54, and 124-125). Ask people to consider:

- What parts of life are the hardest for you to accept?

ASSIGNMENT FOR NEXT WEEK

- Read *Lesson II: Unconditionally Choose to Give.*
- Choose one of the "Ten Ways to Practice Giving Unconditionally" (see pages 58-62) this week. Take note of your feelings about the experience for discussion next week.

WEEK III. *Giving with Authenticity*

OPENING DISCUSSION QUESTIONS

✦ Depending on the size of your group, discuss these questions as one group, or break up into small groups of 2-4 people:

  • How did you choose to unconditionally give to yourself or others this week? Describe your experience and your feelings about it.
  • In your reading of the lesson on unconditional giving, what seemed especially important to you?

ACTIVITY

✦ Have participants take the Quick Quiz "How Does the Martyr Affect You" on pages 66-67 and score it. Discuss the interpretation of the results.

✦ Discuss these questions (as one group or in smaller groups):

  • What situations ask you to give in ways that are difficult for you?
  • What do you consider to be your unique traits?

✦ Present *authenticity* as a way to decrease the influence of the Martyr (see pages 19, 65, 79, 86-92, and 124). Ask people to think about their unique traits and consider:

  • What is something that comes easily to you that you can or have shared to help others?

ASSIGNMENT FOR NEXT WEEK

  • Look at the list of expectations on pages 75-76. Does any of them sound like you?
  • Read *Lesson III: Integrate Your Unique Gifts.*
  • Choose one of the "Ten Ways to Practice Giving Authentically" (see pages 86-92) this week. Take note of your feelings about the experience for discussion next week.

WEEK IV. *Giving with Joy*

OPENING DISCUSSION QUESTIONS
⬠ Depending on the size of your group, discuss these questions as one group, or break up into small groups of 2-4 people:

- How did you choose to give authentically this week? Describe your experience and your feelings about it.
- In your reading on integrating your unique gifts, what seemed especially important to you?

ACTIVITY
⬠ Have participants take the Quick Quiz "How Does the Controller Affect You" on pages 96-97 and score it. Discuss the interpretation of the results.

⬠ Discuss the following (as one group or in smaller groups):

- Think of a present giving situation in your life. What results help you feel that your efforts are worthwhile? How important are these results to you? What makes you feel good about your giving in this situation, regardless of what happens?

⬠ Present *appreciation* as a way to decrease the influence of the Controller (see pages 19, 104, and 125). Ask people to consider:

- Can you think of a problematic situation that you tried hard to control or fix and then, when you finally let go, a solution presented itself?

ASSIGNMENT FOR NEXT WEEK
- Read *Lesson IV: Delight in the Act of Giving* and *Lesson V: Experience the Expanding Capacity to Give.*
- Choose one of the "Ten Ways to Practice Joyful Giving" (see pages 108-114) this week. Take note of your feelings about the experience for discussion next week.

WEEK V. *The Growing Giving Heart*

OPENING DISCUSSION QUESTIONS

☙ Depending on the size of your group, discuss these questions as one group, or break up into small groups of 2-4 people:

- How did your choice to give this week increase your pleasure in an act of giving? Describe your experience and your feelings about it.
- In your reading about the joy of giving and expanding your giving, what seemed especially important to you?

ACTIVITY

☙ Break into small groups of 2-4 persons. Direct each group to invite one person at a time to share their thoughts about one of the following:

- If you are currently in a depleting giving situation, how can you turn it into a replenishing one?
- How would you like to expand your acts of giving, either to yourself or to others, at work, home, leisure, in volunteering, etc.
- How will you nurture your giving?

CLOSING

☙ Take time for evaluation and feedback.

APPENDIX B
Suggestions for Church Groups

If you are using this book with volunteers from your church,
you may especially want to look at what Scripture
has to say about these aspects of giving.

Format:
A Five Week Course
1 to 1 ½ hours per session.
The time can easily be shortened or lengthened
by varying the number of activities or discussion questions.

WEEK I.   *Giving from your Heart's Desire*

OPENING EXERCISE

↔ Offer ways for people to meet each other.

OPENING DISCUSSION QUESTIONS

↔ Depending on the size of your group, discuss these questions as one group, or break up into small groups of 2-4 people:

- How do you experience giving in your life?
- How is your energy level? Do you feel drained and exhausted by the demands of life or do you feel fairly comfortable with the balance in your life?
- What is your most recent experience of saying "yes" when you really wanted to say "no"?
- What does God about say giving?

ACTIVITY

↔ Have participants take the self-inventory "Do You Need Gifts from Yourself?"on pages 31-32 and score it.

↔ Let the results open up the following discussion questions:

- What did you discover about yourself?
- How hard, or easy, is it for you to give to yourself?
- What interferes or helps?

↔ Present or initiate a discussion on what God tells us about taking care of ourselves, based on 2 Corinthians 8:12-15 and Luke 10:5-9.

The Bible teaches us the importance of balance in our giving. In a letter to the people of Corinth, Paul explains, "This does not mean that to give relief to others you ought to make things difficult for yourselves: it is a question of balancing what happens to be your surplus now against their present need, and one day they may have something to spare that will supply your own need. That is how we strike a balance." (2 Corinthians 8:13-14, *The Jerusalem Bible*)

In other words, we are responsible for making sure our giving does not deplete us.

An equal part of the balance is receiving gifts from others, which Jesus encourages his disciples to do. He tells them to accept the hospitality and food that are offered while performing their missionary work, and to use the nurturing for replenishment so they can continue to give according to their purpose (Luke 10:5-9).

ASSIGNMENT FOR NEXT WEEK

- Read the *Introduction* and *Lesson I: Give Wholly to Yourself*.
- Read Matthew 6:1-4, Luke 6:32-36, and Luke 10:25-37.
- Choose one of the "Ten Simple Ways To Practice Giving to Yourself" (see pages 34-37) this week. Take note of your feelings about the experience for discussion next week.

WEEK II. *Giving Unconditionally*

OPENING DISCUSSION QUESTIONS

↭ Depending on the size of your group, discuss these questions as one group, or break up into small groups of 2-4 people:

- How did you choose to nurture yourself this week?
- How did it affect your ability to give to others?
- In your reading on giving wholly to yourself, what seemed especially important to you?

ACTIVITY

↭ Have everyone take the Quick Quiz "How Does the Trader Affect You?" on pages 40-41 and score it. Discuss the interpretation of the results.

↭ Discuss these questions (as one group or in smaller groups):

- Have you ever been in a situation where you felt you gave more than your fair share?
- Have you ever been in a situation where you did not get back what you expected?

↭ Present the idea of *acceptance* as a way to decrease the influence of the Trader (see pages 19, 50-54, and 124-125). Ask people to consider:

- What parts of life are the hardest for you to accept?

↭ Present or initiate a discussion on what God tells us about acceptance and unconditional giving, based on Matthew 6:1-4, Luke 6:32-36, and Luke 10:25-37:

> If we look at the model set by Jesus in the New Testament, we see over and over again the encouragement to give unconditionally, without expectation for recognition: "When you give to the needy, do not let your left

hand know what your right hand is doing so that your giving may be in secret" (Matthew 6:3-4, *NRSV*). When we give in "secret," we know our actions are not driven by the motives of praise from others. Jesus asks us to give to our enemies freely, to lend expecting nothing in return (Luke 6: 32-36).

Perhaps the classic illustration of this is the story of the "Good Samaritan" (Luke 10:25-37) in which a man from Samaria followed his heart's urging. He stopped to help a needy Jewish man (considered the enemy to the Samaritans at that time), with no hope or expectation of payback.

ASSIGNMENT FOR NEXT WEEK

- Read *Lesson II: Unconditionally Choose to Give.*
- Read Exodus 35:4-36 and 1 Corinthians 12:4-30.
- Choose one of the "Ten Ways to Practice Giving Unconditionally" (see pages 58-62) this week. Take note of your feelings about the experience for discussion next week.

WEEK III. *Giving with Authenticity*

OPENING DISCUSSION QUESTIONS

⮑ Depending on the size of your group, discuss these questions as one group, or break up into small groups of 2-4 people:

- How did you choose to unconditionally give to yourself or others this week? Describe your experience and your feelings about it.
- In your reading of the lesson on unconditional giving, what seemed especially important to you?

ACTIVITY

⮑ Have participants take the Quick Quiz "How Does the Martyr Affect You" on pages 66-67 and score it. Discuss the interpretation of the results.

⮑ Discuss these questions (as one group or in smaller groups):

- What situations ask you to give in ways that are difficult for you?
- What do you consider to be your unique traits?

⮑ Present *authenticity* as a way to decrease the influence of the Martyr (see pages 19, 65, 79, 86-92. and 124). Ask people to think about their unique traits and consider:

- What is something that comes easily to you that you can share or have shared to help others?

⮑ Present or initiate a discussion on what God tells us about authentic gifts, based on Exodus 35:4-36 and 1 Corinthians 12:4-30:

Recognizing individuality and diversity of gifts is a familiar theme in Scripture. In the Old Testament, the importance of recognizing our natural gifts and including them in our acts of giving is illustrated in the building of God's tabernacle related in Exodus 35:4-36. Moses asked that only those with "willing spirit" (*NRSV*) contribute to the endeavor. Following their hearts' desires, the people gave according to their abilities and talents. Gifts ranged from gold and fine linen to stone-cutting and woodcarving—but whatever the talent or offering, all was given with a generous and open heart.

In the New Testament, Paul emphasizes the need for each person to discover their own gifts, rather than attempting to give according to a way that they perceive as "greater," and he reaffirms that we each need to honor our unique gifts:

"There is a variety of gifts but always the same Spirit; there are all sorts of service to be done, but always to the same Lord, working in all sorts of different ways in different people." (1 Corinthians 12:4-6, *The Jerusalem Bible*)

ASSIGNMENT FOR NEXT WEEK

- Look at the list of expectations on pages 75-76. Does any of them sound like you?
- Read *Lesson III: Integrate Your Unique Gifts.*
- Read John 6:1-13, Mark 12:41-44, and 2 Corinthians 9:6-15.
- Choose one of the "Ten Ways to Practice Giving Authentically" (see pages 86-92) this week. Take note of your feelings about the experience for discussion next week.

WEEK IV. *Giving with Joy*

OPENING DISCUSSION QUESTIONS

⬠ Depending on the size of your group, discuss these questions as one group, or break up into small groups of 2-4 people:

- How did you choose to give authentically this week? Describe your experience and your feelings about it.
- In your reading on integrating your unique gifts, what seemed especially important to you?

ACTIVITY

⬠ Have participants take the Quick Quiz "How Does the Controller Affect You" on pages 96-97 and score it. Discuss the interpretation of the results.

⬠ Discuss the following (as one group or in smaller groups):

- Think of a present giving situation in your life. What results help you feel that your efforts are worthwhile? How important are these results to you? What makes you feel good about your giving in this situation, regardless of what happens?

⬠ Present *appreciation* as a way to decrease the influence of the Controller (see pages 19, 104, and 125). Ask people to consider:

- Can you think of a problematic situation that you tried hard to control or fix and then, when you finally let go, a solution presented itself?

⬠ Present or initiate a discussion on what God tells us about appreciation, based on John 6:1-13, Mark 12:41-44, and 2 Corinthians 9:6-15:

The boy who gave Jesus his five loaves of bread and two fish is a story that shows the power of a gift motivated by faith in the act of giving itself rather than a need to control the outcome. Even though it seemed as if such a small amount of food could not possibly satisfy the hunger of thousands, this boy's gift produced a miraculous outcome.

The story of the widow who gave her last two small copper coins reported in Mark 12:41-44 further illustrates gifts that come from a true desire to give rather than a need to control the gift's effects.

In his words to the Corinthians (2 Corinthians 9:6-15), Paul compares the farmer who plants generously and gets an abundant crop to the one who plants sparingly and produces only a few crops, showing us that the gifts which multiply are those given freely from the heart.

ASSIGNMENT FOR NEXT WEEK

- Read *Lesson IV: Delight in the Act of Giving* and *Lesson V: Experience the Expanding Capacity to Give.*
- Read 1 Corinthians 13.
- Choose one of the "Ten Ways to Practice Joyful Giving" (see pages 108-114) this week. Take note of your feelings about the experience for discussion next week.

WEEK V. *The Growing Giving Heart*

OPENING DISCUSSION QUESTIONS

ᗍ Depending on the size of your group, discuss these questions as one group, or break up into small groups of 2-4 people:

- How did your choice to give this week increase your pleasure in an act of giving? Describe your experience and your feelings about it.
- In your reading about the joy of giving and expanding your giving, what seemed especially important to you?

ACTIVITY

ᗍ Present or initiate a discussion on what God tells us about giving more, based on 1 Corinthians 13:

As we are reminded by Paul in his letter to the Corinthians, even the most magnificent gifts or supreme sacrifices mean nothing unless motivated by love:

"If I give away all that I possess, piece by piece, and if I even let them take my body to burn it, but am without love, it will do me no good whatever." (1 Corinthians 13:3, *The Jerusalem Bible*)

ᗍ Break into small groups of 2-4 persons. Direct each group to invite one person at a time to share their thoughts about one of the following:

- If you are currently in a depleting giving situation, how can you turn it into a replenishing one?
- How would you like to expand your acts of giving, either to yourself or to others, at work, at home, in the church?
- How will you nurture your giving?

✜ You may want to pass out a list of opportunities at the church and let people consider where the church's needs match their authentic gifts.

CLOSING

✜ Take time for evaluation and feedback.

APPENDIX C
The Giving Bag
(B.Y.O.B.: "Bring Your Own Bag")

Giving to others often requires waiting. For example, a caregiver of a family member with a serious illness may spend hours a week in waiting rooms. Did you know that waiting can be good for the soul? By creating *The Giving Bag*, you can replenish yourself while caring for others. Fill your tote with items that offer you comfort and pleasure and speak to your unique desires. *The Giving Bag* is the gift that keeps on giving. Choose a carrying bag that speaks to your authentic nature and fill it with items such as:

- Your own special cup for coffee or tea
- Mints, gum, or hard candy
- An energy bar
- Chocolate
- Flavored lip balm, tissues, and hand lotion
- CD player or tape-recorder with a headset, and favorite music or a relaxation tape
- Sketch pad and colored pencils or markers
- Journal
- Small photo album with favorite pictures and/or inspiring quotes
- A card, couple of sheets of stationery and envelope for writing a letter
- A favorite book or magazine/crossword puzzles, word games
- Bottle of water
- A small teddy bear or favorite stuffed animal

Take *The Giving Bag* along with you the next time you anticipate spending some time waiting. You may be surprised to discover that when the receptionist informs you that there has been a delay, you may feel a "jump for joy" deep inside because your soul has been given a little extra time to play!

❧

To remind you of the ideas in this book, we have created a matching "Giving Bag." Adorned with a silk-screened imprint of artist Sara Steele's beautiful watercolor painting "Hollyhocks with Sunspots / Freedom Flowers" from the cover of the book, this natural-colored canvas tote bag carries the inspiring message *"Give to Your Heart's Content."*

For more information, contact:
Linda R. Harper, Ph.D.
708-423-5330
lharper6@aol.com
   or
Sara Steele
215-242-4107
sara@sara/steele.com
http://www.sarasteele.com/
   or
Innisfree Press
800-367-5872
InnisfreeP@aol.com
www.InnisfreePress.com

Notes

LESSON I: *Give Wholly to Yourself*

1. Northrup, Christiane. *Women's Bodies, Women's Wisdom: Creating Physical and Emotional Health and Healing.* (New York: Bantam Books, 1998), 599. Reprinted by permission of Random House, Inc., Bantam Books Permissions Department.

2. Golden, Stephanie. *Slaying the Mermaid: Women and the Culture of Sacrifice.* (New York: Harmony Books, 1998), v.

3. *Ibid.*, 21.

4. Kipnis, Aaron R. *Knights Without Armor: A Practical Guide for Men in Quest of Masculine Soul.* (New York: Jeremy P. Tarcher/ Putnam Books, 1991), 15. Reprinted by permission of the author.

5. *Ibid,* 40.

6. Moore, Thomas. *Care of the Soul: A Guide for Cultivating Depth and Sacredness in Everyday Life.* (New York: HarperCollins, 1992), 74. Copyright © 1992 by Thomas Moore. Reprinted by permission of HarperCollins Publishers Inc.

7. L'Engle, Madeleine. *And It Was Good: Reflections on Beginnings.* (Wheaton, IL: Harold Shaw Publishers, 1983), 21.

8. L'Engle, Madeleine. *A Stone for a Pillow.* (Wheaton, IL: Harold Shaw Publishers, 1986), 42.

9. Chödrön, Pema. *Start Where You Are: A Guide to Compassionate Living.* (Boston: Shambhala Publications, 1994), 33. Copyright © 1994 by Pema Chödrön. Reprinted by arrangement with Shambhala Publications, Inc., www.shambhala.com.

10. Peck, M. Scott. *The Road Less Traveled: A New Psychology of Love, Traditional Values and Spiritual Growth.* (New York: Simon and Schuster, 1978), 15.

11. Lesser, Elizabeth. *The New American Spirituality: A Seeker's Guide.* (New York: Random House, 1999), 192. Copyright © 1999 by Elizabeth Lesser. Reprinted by permission of Random House, Inc..

12. Nouwen, Henri. *Reaching Out: The Three Movements of the Spiritual Life.* (New York: Doubleday, 1966), 39-40. Reprinted by permission of Random House, Inc., Doubleday Permissions Department.

13. *Ibid.,* 30.

14. Moore, Thomas. *Care of the Soul,* xi.

15. *Ibid.,* 166.

16. Books about the simple joys of life include Vienne, Veronique, *The Art of Doing Nothing: Simple Ways to Make Time for Yourself;* Frakes, Mary H. Mindwalks, *100 Easy Ways to Relieve Stress, Stay Motivated, and Nourish Your Soul;* Capellini, Steve, *The Royal Treatment: How You Can Take Home the Pleasure of the Great Luxury Spas;* Louden, Jennifer, *The Woman's Comfort Book: A Self Nurturing Guide for Restoring Balance in Your Life;* Oliver, Stephanie Stokes S., *Daily Cornbread: 365 Secrets for a Healthy Mind, Body and Soul;* St. James, Elaine, *Living the Simple Life: A Guide to Scaling Down and Enjoying More.*

LESSON II: Unconditionally Choose to Give

17. Kushner, Rabbi Harold, "To Love and Be Loved," in *Handbook for the Heart,* edited by Richard Carlson and Benjamin Shield, 1996 (Boston, New York: Little, Brown and Company), 35.

18. Tzu, Lao. *Tao Te Ching.* A New English Version with Foreword and Notes by Stephen Mitchell, translation copyright © 1988 by Stephen Mitchell. Reprinted by permission of HarperCollins Publishers Inc.

LESSON III: Integrate Your Unique Gifts

19. *Ibid.*

LESSON IV: Delight in the Act of Giving

20. *Tao Te Ching/Lao Tsu.* Translation by Gia-Fu Feng and Jane English. New York: Vintage Books, 1989), 29.

21. Levoy, Gregg. *Callings: Finding and Following an Authentic Life* (New York: Harmony Books, 1997), 11. Reprinted by permission of Random House, Inc.

Bibliography

Carlson, Richard and Benjamin Shield, eds. *Handbook for the Heart.* Boston, New York: Little, Brown and Company, 1996.

Chödrön, Pema. *Start Where You Are: A Guide to Compassionate Living.* Boston: Shambhala Publications, 1994.

Golden, Stephanie. *Slaying the Mermaid: Women and the Culture of Sacrifice.* New York: Harmony Books, 1998.

Keenan, Paul. *Stages of the Soul: The Path of the Soulful Life.* Chicago: Contemporary Books, 2000.

Kipnis, Aaron R. *Knights Without Armor: A Practical Guide for Men in Quest of Masculine Soul.* New York: Jeremy P. Tarcher/Putnam Books, 1991.

L'Engle, Madeleine. *And It Was Good: Reflections on Beginnings.* Wheaton, IL: Harold Shaw Publishers, 1983.

_____. *A Stone for a Pillow.* Wheaton, IL: Harold Shaw Publishers, 1986.

Lesser, Elizabeth. *The New American Spirituality: A Seeker's Guide.* New York: Random House, 1999.

Levoy, Gregg. *Callings: Finding and Following an Authentic Life.* New York: Harmony Books, 1997.

Moore, Thomas. *Care of the Soul: A Guide for Cultivating Depth and Sacredness in Everyday Life.* New York: HarperCollins, 1992.

Northrup, Christiane. *Women's Body, Women's Wisdom: Creating Physical and Emotional Health and Healing.* New York: Bantam Books, 1998.

Nouwen, Henri. *Reaching Out: The Three Movements of the Spiritual Life.* New York: Doubleday, 1966.

Peck, M. Scott. *The Road Less Traveled: A New Psychology of Love, Traditional Values and Spiritual Growth.* New York: Simon and Schuster, 1978.

Tzu, Lao. *Tao Te Ching.* A New English Version with Foreword and Notes by Stephen Mitchell. New York: Harper and Row, 1988.

About the Author

*L*INDA R. HARPER, PH.D., is a clinical psychologist and workshop leader who has been in private practice in the Chicago area for over eighteen years. In addition to her newest book, *Give to Your Heart's Content . . . Without Giving Yourself Away*, she is the author of *The Tao of Eating: Feeding Your Soul through Everyday Experiences with Food* (Innisfree Press, 1998).

Dr. Harper has lead workshops at the International Association of Eating Disorders Professionals (IAEDP) national symposium, the National Association for the Advancement of Fat Acceptance (NAAFA) conference, and the Annual Women's Wellness Workshop in Chicago. She has also lectured at academic and medical institutions and public libraries throughout the Chicago area, as well as the American University in Paris. Dr. Harper has conducted numerous radio and television interviews, and feature stories about her first book, *The Tao of Eating*, have appeared in *Fitness, Women's Sports & Fitness,* and *Natural Health* magazines, and in newspapers across the country.

Innisfree classics that call to the deep heart's core . . .

A GUIDE TO
SOULFUL
EATING
*The Tao of
Eating*
*Feeding Your Soul
through Everyday
Experiences
with Food*
by Linda R. Harper

NAMED ONE OF
THE BEST
SPIRITUAL
BOOKS OF THE
YEAR
Red Fire
*A Quest for
Awakening*
by Paula D'Arcy

BOOKS THAT
TOUCH THE
DEEPEST CORE
OF THE
FEMININE
*Circle of
Stones* and
*I Sit
Listening to
the Wind*
by Judith
Duerk

UNDERSTAND
YOUR
RELATIONSHIP
WITH MONEY
*A Woman's Book
of Money &
Spiritual Vision*
*Putting Your Finan-
cial Values into Spiri-
tual Perspective*
by Rosemary
Williams

NEW
INSPIRATION
FROM A
WOMAN'S
CLASSIC
*Return
to the Sea*
*Reflections on Anne
Morrow Lindbergh's
"Gift from the Sea"*
by Anne M. Johnson

A BOOK TO
READ IF YOU
DON'T HAVE
ENOUGH TIME
TO READ !
Sabbath Sense
*A Spiritual Antidote
for the Overworked*
by Donna Schaper

Published by Innisfree Press ~ 800-367-5872 ~ *www.InnisfreePress.com*
Available from bookstores everywhere. Call for a free catalog.